THE RICHES OF JESUS CHRIST

The Plan of God to Enrich His People is Now!

Enow Thomas

Copyright © 2022 by **Enow Thomas**

Paperback ISBN: 978-1-952098-93-2

Printed in the United States of America. All rights reserved solely by the publisher. This book or parts thereof may not be reproduced in any form, stored in a retrieval system, or transmitted in any form by any means - electronic, mechanical, photocopy. Unless otherwise noted, Bible quotations are taken from the Holy Bible, New King James Version (NKJV) Copyright 1982 by Thomas Nelson, Inc., publishers. Used by permission.

Cornerstone Publishing

A Division of Cornerstone Creativity Group LLC
Phone: +1(516) 547-4999
info@thecornerstonepublishers.com
www.thecornerstonepublishers.com

For books and media resources or to schedule the author for speaking, engagements, contact

cantact24btv@gamil.com
Whatsapp+33601750056
paypal.me/bloodtvfrance
WWW.BLOODTV.FR

CONTENTS

Introduction..5

Chapter 1: Are You Ready?............................9

Chapter 2: You Are Special..........................15

Chapter 3: You Are A Blessing....................21

Chapter 4: Wrapped In The Word..............41

Chapter 5: You Are Still On Track..............49

Chapter 6: The Pilgrim's Progress...............55

Chapter 7: Decrypting God's Voice............63

Chapter 8: "How Do I Hear From God?"..............75

Chapter 9: Benefit Of Studying God's Word............83

Chapter 10: Who Knows Tomorrow?.......95

Chapter 11: Keeper Of Covenants............103

Conclusion..113

INTRODUCTION

The Bible is not just a collection of stories, tales, events, and spiritual experiences of people and how they walked with God. It is not just a book of laws and commandments that you must obey as children of God. It is not just a book that contains some mighty moves of God and how He displays His power and dominion over man. Beyond all that, the Bible is a compilation of God's plan and purpose for His children, and that includes YOU.

He has great plans for you, and He has inspired great men by the Holy Spirit to write them in a way you can comprehend and relate with. Interestingly, one of His golden plans is to enrich you. Yes. I know you may think this doesn't sound like a Holy statement, or perhaps you have been told that poverty is synonymous with holiness. Today, I want to tell you God desires and has made provisions for you to be super-wealthy.

He said in 3 John 1:2, *"Beloved, I wish above all things that thou mayest prosper and be in health, even as thy soul prospereth."* In other words, God is saying, although I wish that you live in health, I wish that you get promoted in your career, I wish that you get married, I wish that you have a child of your own. However, above all, I desire to see you become a man and a woman of wealth.

God has planned from the earth's foundation to ensure that you aren't struggling to make ends meet, nor are you struggling to survive because the economy is unstable. From the beginning, before He created the first man, Adam, He already created everything He will ever need. Do you observe that all through man's stay in the Garden of Eden, there was no time He asked God for a need? Why? Eden was a place of abundance, a place of plenty and sufficiency. And that's God's desire for you also.

Furthermore, the Bible refers to Jesus, the savior of the world in 2 Corinthians 8:9, *"For ye know the grace of our Lord Jesus Christ, that, though he was rich, yet for your sakes he became poor, that ye through his poverty might be rich."* Did you catch that? Jesus didn't just come to save you from sin and leave you in poverty and impoverished; neither did He die just to wash your sins away and give you a new heart to serve God. Emphatic No. He also came to bless and increase you. See what the Bible says in Act 3:26, *"Unto you first God, having raised up his Son Jesus, sent him to bless you, in turning away every one of you from his iniquities."* Jesus came to bless you in addition to washing your sins away. Isn't that amazing?

However, you may ask but why are things still hard for me? Why do I still struggle to pay my bills? Why is debt choking me up, and I can't even boast of any savings or investments? The truth is God is a God of order. Andy Stanley once said, *"God is a God of systems and predictability and order, and God honors planning."*

That God He has plans for you means doesn't mean it will jump at you suddenly. There is always a process. And this is where most Christians miss out. They think it has to happen right now; they start to time God and compare themselves with others. And when it doesn't happen when they intend, they seek alternatives and give up on God.

But I want to tell you that God's plan for you is not a lie; however, it will only take the hand of God to fulfill His plan. Everything in life, including your life, happens within God's perfect plan. He makes all things beautiful in His time. So, you have to trust Him and trust His timing.

On your path to fulfilling God's plan, you may face challenges and temptations that seek to discourage you from following God and push you to settle for less. Yes, many great men that God has blessed and enriched in scriptures also went through a similar experience. The journey may be unpleasant sometimes, but you just have to maintain your way before God. Take a cue from the life of Job, who lost everything he had in one day, and God had plans to give him double what he had before. But the journey to that double wasn't a sweet memory to behold. But he stayed on.

So, get set, as I share with you some truth about God's plan for your life and how you can maintain stability, patience, and perseverance, which are vital qualities to enjoying the fullness of God's plan for your life.

Join me in a journey into your wealthy place? Let's dive in!

CHAPTER 1

ARE YOU READY?

Friend, your choice to read this book is the best decision you could have made at such a time as this. You see, the Lord revealed to me the purposes for which He has called us to be His followers. The truth is, many people are living this Christian life as a defeated people. And most of the people they have turned to condemn those doing fine and successful. Many people have turned to condemn them and speak against them because they have looked into their lives and realized how far they have gone. They are not succeeding. They are not going ahead, but the Lord has explained to me the reasons why he called everyone to be his follower. The plan of God is for us to inherit blessings and every good thing of life both physically and in the spirit because that is the reason the Lord Jesus had to die for us.

And the way He has planned for us to achieve these things is very easy. They are not complicated. But you need understanding. You must seek for understanding of the way because the ways of God are higher than man. So, the revelation from this book is going to open your heart to new dimensions of truth and insight. It will open your eyes to know exactly why you are a Christian, why you are following Jesus, attending your church, and why you are praying. It contains lights that are vital to our walk with God.

Now, when we preach, or we are called through evangelization or through revelation to be Christians, know that from that moment and from that day that you accept Christ as your Lord and Savior, your name is already registered as one of those that have life in Christ. You are saved. It means that you have achieved everything in life. From the day that you accepted the Lord, Jesus Christ, you have achieved everything that a man might have been in need of on this earth in the physical, in the spiritual, until eternal life. That is the purpose that he did what he went through, the cross, the grief, the resurrection, and the ascendance.

And so there has not been lots of emphasis on how a Christian can obtain what the Father has already prepared them. So, the first thing that we must do is to begin to study it to hear the voice of God. You must learn how to hear the voice of God. The way God communicates, God communicates in certain ways that if you are in the spirit, you understand that this is God speaking. I will explain this later in this book. Also, you will learn how to work with the angels because the angels do not operate the same way the Lord operates. They are different because God sends angels, and there are certain times that God acts in your life.

For example, the first thing to know as a Christian, but from the first day that you become a Christian, that is you confessed with your mouth, and you believe in your heart that Jesus Christ is your Lord and Savior. So, what is happening is that your life is gone. Your old life is gone in Christ. It means that Christ now governs anything now that happens in your life. The Bible says in Romans 13:14, *"But put ye on the Lord Jesus Christ, and make not provision for the flesh, to fulfill the lusts thereof."* Also, the scripture says in Ephesians 4:22-24, *"That ye put off concerning the former conversation the old man, which is corrupt according to the deceitful lusts; And be renewed in the spirit of your mind; And that ye put on the new man, which after God is created in righteousness and true holiness."*

So as a Christian, anything that you are going through, God is not oblivious of it. God is aware because He is the all-knowing God. He knows what you're going through, but you don't have to be negligent. You have to be active. Active in the things of God, active in prayer, and also active in fasting. He has plans for you despite how it has been.

Why? Because you have entered into a new life that puts you at an advantage over the issues of life. A life of favor. Because the things of God, are not physical. The things of God are spiritually discerned and can't be understood by the human mind. So, what I was saying is that if you are not fasting, reading the Word, praying, doing God's works, it will be difficult for you to hear the voice of God because God is Spirit. God is right here, but you can find Him in the spiritual dimension. In some special cases, God can arise, while He can come right into the physical realm in certain operations. But it is good for you as a spiritual person to always be alert, through praying, and fasting, attending church, and doing God's work.

So now, when you become a Christian, the Lord will create certain situations and challenges which will be the avenue that God would use to bless you. Yes, because certain things will happen in your life when you become a Christian. It is through these challenges that you will achieve your blessing. That means that you pass your exam well, you have everything to eat well, and you have a good job. Now, things are going to be challenging. For instance, you could be kidnapped. You couldn't lose some of your articles. You know, you could be arrested by the police. There are many things that could happen in your life, even though you are a Christian. But understand that all these are for your good.

You can also be accused of certain things you didn't even do. I mean that there are things turning around you, negative or positive. All these are for the purposes and the plan of God to accomplish in your life. The Bible is replete with great men and women of God that fulfilled the purpose of God in their generation, yet they had their share of unexpected and unpleasant experiences on the verge of fulfilling God's purpose for their lives.

That is what God has used to inspire me to write this

book. Your Father wants me to tell you not to give up but hold firm to His plan for your life. No discovery in life is more glorious than finding out God's ultimate purpose for your life. I'm sure you are ready to know more about your life beyond what your eyes can see.

CHAPTER 2

YOU ARE SPECIAL

We live in a time when unhealthy comparison has permeated our environment. Most people spend time online swapping their phones from one social media platform to another. They follow successes, flashy cars, beautiful mansions, cute stature, and wonder why they are so unlucky. They wonder why they aren't as successful as their social media influencer; they wonder why they can't afford the lifestyle they see online. They look at their stature and dislike themselves for not having the opportunities others have.

Have you ever felt like a failure in life? Have you ever felt insecure about your appearance, skill, abilities, personality, or achievements? Have you ever felt worthless and less important? Have you ever said to yourself, "I am not attractive? I can't do the things the other person can do. I am not good enough. Nothing good can ever happen in my life. I am a failure." Too often, we confess such a self-limiting mindset, and before long, our life begins to go down like a rock tossed into the ocean.

I want you to understand that you are special. As a child of God, you are not an accidental discharge but a deliberate creature on the earth. God created you especially without outsourcing any part of your creation. The Bible says in Genesis 1:26, *"And God said, let us make man in our image, after our likeness: and let them have dominion over the fish of the sea, and over the fowl of the air, and over the cattle, and overall the earth, and over every creeping thing that creepeth upon the earth."* Did you catch that? This verse means you were created in God's image and perfect likeness. He didn't place anyone by the side as a template to form you. Guess what, He put His own image as a template by the side. He created you as His masterpiece and not a carbon copy of anyone else. That's how unique you are.

Also, of all the creation of God, you are the only one with a living soul. Why? Check this out; Genesis 2:7 says, *"And the LORD God formed man of the dust of the ground and breathed into his nostrils the breath of life; and man became a living soul."* This goes to show that God deposited a part of Himself into you. His life is inside you. That means you have a supernatural nature that is immune to any earthly limitations. So, what affects others cannot affect you. Where others are limited by nature, you have a superior nature with an ability to overcome and escape. Do you now see that you are special?

Our inability to see ourselves as God sees us is the prick that draws us back from stretching to our fullness. When you don't have a revelation of how God sees you, you settle for what society calls you. You start to see yourself from the lens of others and this places a limitation on your colorful destiny. But I believe that because you are holding this book, the transformation has begun. Now let me expose to you further from God's word why I said you are special.

Check out what God's word says about you in 1 Peter 2:9 (KJV): *"But ye are a chosen generation, a royal priesthood, an holy nation, a peculiar people; that ye should shew forth the praises of him who hath called you out of darkness into his marvelous light"* You are royalty. Can you believe that about yourself? You are not a mediocre, but you belong to a royal family. After redemption, you are taken from slavery to royalty. Psalms 113:7 He raiseth up the poor out of the dust, and leftish the needy out of the dunghill; Psalms 113:8 That he may set him with princes, even with the princes of his people.

Your Father is the King of Kings, and as a child of God through the blood of Jesus, you can't be anything less than a Prince of the highest. Now let me take you deeper. The bible says the earth is the Lord and the fullness. And God owns the heaven and the earth, and since there can't be two kings in heaven, He has designated the earth for you to reign. So, you are a king not just prince. Revelations 5:9-10 says, *"And they sung a new song, saying, Thou art worthy to take the book, and to open the seals thereof: for thou wast slain, and hast redeemed us to God by thy blood out of every kindred, and tongue, and people, and nation; And hast made us unto our God kings and priests: and we shall reign on the earth."* Awesome!

With these revelations, do you still think you should

be comparing yourself with others? Do you still think anyone is better than you? Do you still think you need anyone's approval? I don't think so.

What more? Jesus also pointed to your uniqueness in His sermon on the mount. He said in Matthew 5:13-16, *"Ye are the salt of the earth: but if the salt have lost his savour, wherewith shall it be salted? it is thenceforth good for nothing, but to be cast out, and to be trodden under foot of men. Ye are the light of the world. A city that is set on a hill cannot be hid. Neither do men light a candle, and put it under a bushel, but on a candlestick; and it giveth light unto all that are in the house. Let your light so shine before men, that they may see your good works, and glorify your Father which is in heaven."* Do you understand where you come in? You have a global destiny, not a local destiny. You are a star to be looked at and a reference point for all, and not mediocre.

Jesus said lights should be placed on the candlestick to give light to everyone in the house. That is, you are a solution in this dark world, not a part of the problem. You are here to solve human challenges. People should look up to you, not look down at you. Simply put, you are special.

While you may think you are not a genius and can't do what others are doing, I want to tell you that Christ shared His mind with you. The Bible says in 1 Corinthians 2:16, *"For who hath known the mind of the Lord, that he may instruct him? But we have the mind of Christ."* You have the mind of Christ. That is, you have the divine ability and supernatural intellect that is beyond what can be learned in any high school or university. You have what it takes to proffer solutions that only the Spirit of God can teach a man.

You see, God is jealous of you. He said in Zechariah 2:8, *"For thus saith the LORD of hosts; After the glory hath he sent me unto the nations which spoiled you: for he that toucheth you toucheth the apple of his eye.* This is the most fantastic statement from God to you. You are the apple of His eye. Let me make you understand. The eye is designed with a closing system whenever anything wants to enter. That's how protected you are. God says, you are that special and unique to Him. No disease can touch you, no sickness can afflict you, you can't suffer what others suffer. You are a precious entity.

Friend, I had to expose to you how special you are because you cannot maximize the plans and purpose of God for your life unless you first know who you are in Christ. You can't keep making cheap comparisons and still be all that God want's you to be. You can't be that millionaire that God has proposed when you compare yourself with people who struggle and steal to make money. In order to experience all that God has for us, you need to understand who the Lord says you are.

You need to know that every situation you are going through that seems like God is not there is just His way to show forth and manifest His power in your life. He knows the plans He has for you; they are special.

So, wake up every day and study God's word, which contains His plan and description of your life. Don't define your life by your background anymore or the color of your skin but by God's word. See yourself as unique. You may not have started manifesting the fullness of His glory yet but know that you have a glorious destiny. The Bible says in Romans 8:29-30, *"For whom he did foreknow, he also did predestinate to be conformed to the image of his Son, that he might be the firstborn among many brethren. Moreover, whom he did predestinate, them he also called: and whom he called, them he also justified: and whom he justified, them he also glorified."*

Your end is glorious, and you must first see yourself as that. Because until you see what God has planned for you, He may not manifest it in your life. The bible says in Jeremiah 1:11-12, *"Moreover the word of the LORD came unto me, saying, Jeremiah, what seest thou? And I said, I see a rod of an almond tree.* Then said the LORD unto me, Thou hast well seen: for I will hasten my word to perform it." God will quickly fulfill His plan to enrich you, which He has ordained for you if you first see it. Despite where you are, you must see yourself giving to may. You must see yourself lending to many people and a blessing to nations.

You are special, and that's who you are.

CHAPTER 3

YOU ARE A BLESSING

You see, you are not just special, but a blessing. Yes, you are a blessing to your community, your family, and your nation. That is God's plan for you. He didn't save you so you could suffer again, but you could be a blessing to many. He wasn't you to be like Job, who said in Job 29:15-17, *"I was eyes to the blind, and feet was I to the lame. I was a father to the poor: and the cause which I knew not I searched out. And I brake the jaws of the wicked, and plucked the spoil out of his teeth."* He was a source of joy to many people. That is God's plan for you.

Irrespective of your background and upbringing, you are enough. God can use you to cause a global change and restore peace in the lives of others.

Now let me share this humbling example with you. I'm going to use the life of Naaman. Naaman, an Old Testament leader was the second in command in the nation of Syria. He was very victorious in his endeavors, but the Bible says that it was God that gave him power, but Naaman didn't know the God of Israel. Still, God gave an unbeliever power, wisdom, a lot of things that permitted him to win his wars because Syria was dominating during those days.

So, what happened is that in Israel, they came to Israel and captured some girls as slaves back to Syria. And it happened that one of the girls was sent to the house of Naaman. Now the girl and the family of the girl thought that it was a curse. They felt misfortune had befallen them. Or how do you explain a girl that had dreams and aspirations, now a slave in another land? The enemy has attacked them. And maybe they have done wrong somewhere. They began to say, how can this happen? How come it's my daughter that was kidnapped.

Interestingly, the Bible didn't mention the name of this girl. Yet, we can say that she is one of the few people that lived in the divine plan for their lives.

This girl is one of the girls that accomplished her mission very successfully. When she got to Syria, she happened to work as a maid to the wife of Naaman. It looks like a coincidence, but I tell you that God has actually been planning all these for a long time. The plan was the plan of God. The plan of God was to reveal himself to Naaman as the one and true God, and taking up this young lady as his maid was the first step

But what is my point? It is about the girl. The girl was captured and taken to Syria, but it was for a mission and not luxury. You see, I wish every believer can understand that you are also on earth for a mission. Or let me put it this way, you are in that office on a mission. What's your profession? A police officer?

Military personnel? Do you work with the government? Or with a private multinational organization. In any area of your function, wherever you might be today. Maybe it is an uncomfortable situation. Maybe it is a comfortable situation. If you look well, if you pray well, you will see the hand of God at work. You will see that God has caused you to be in that position, in that place for a purpose. So, you need to understand this truth, and this will push you to pray and fast so you can hear the voice of God to understand why you are there.

According to the scripture, if this girl remembers when the master was in trouble, Naaman became sick. But this girl could remember a prophet of God who could help her boss. This means that she was a lady of prayers. Because in those days, the children of Israel were like Christians; they prayed in their houses and in the temple. So, this girl was praying. And when the day arrived for her to act, she acted correctly because she had a mission in that house. It was not that she was blessed to be staying in the prime minister's house of a nation. And having good food and living in a good environment, but the purpose was that she was coming to deliver a message that would liberate her boss. She understood that she was a bridge for Naaman to come to know the God of Israel.

So according to scriptures, Naaman was sick; this girl told the Madame that I know a prophet in my country that can heal your husband. That was the only role that the girl was to play. That was the part she had to play in the life of Naaman. And that was the reason that the girl was captured there. Do you know what happened? Just because of this statement, Naaman arrived in Israel. And as you continue to read the story, you will see that Naaman visited the prophet, and did all that the prophet instructed him to do and Naaman was healed. Then Naaman proclaimed that the God of Israel was the only true God. Through this girl, Naaman was healed, and he knew the true God, the creator of heaven and earth, just through this girl. Just put yourself in her place for a moment.

Now, when Naaman went back to Syria, what happened? The girl was blessed because Naaman was so happy with the God of Israel and Israel's people. When Naaman returned home, what do you think Naaman would do to this girl? Remember that his sickness was severe and incurable. That means Naaman was not even supposed to be in office; he was not supposed to even interact with people anymore but should be kept out of the city, according to the law in those days concerning someone that had leprosy. They must be isolated and quarantined from people.

But this girl became a blessing from a captured girl, from a slave girl to become the solution, not only to the person, to the family of Naaman, the general, but also to the nation of Syria. She became a blessing because the nation and the people of Syria needed the experience and expertise of Naaman regarding the security of the country. He was valuable, and they couldn't afford to lose him, so they were ready to do all to ensure that he was cured and his health was fully restored.

Now, what could have been the reward? What can you imagine to be the girl's reward that was staying with him, because before Naaman even leaves for Israel, he already informed the King that there is a Jewish girl in the house. She told me something that I think I should take seriously, so the King already knew about his planned trip. So as they came back, what can you imagine? I, always ask this, what can you imagine if you were in his position? What would you do to the girl?

So that is the same image. And that is the same story that God wants to use you in this generation because many people are blessed. It is good to have blessed them. Many people are blessed who are billionaires, and some are millionaires. They are operating like Naaman, without knowing the God that has blessed them, empowered them, gave them their political powers, and gave them business powers, and the money. They don't know.

So now they are giving thanks to another god. They are giving thanks because Naaman himself confessed that he thought that it was the God of his King that have given him this success. So many people in this country and across the world God blesses, and they know that. God has blessed them; God wants them to know through you that he is the one that has blessed them. There are many people in this nation that the God of Israel has blessed, yet they do not know God, neither do they know the purpose for which God has blessed them. They forget that God has blessed them because of others and not for themselves alone.

Do you now understand that you are a conduit of God's blessing on the earth? Now, let's examine another example from the scriptures of a man who knew his purpose and lived for it. He is a man named Joseph.

Almost all Christians must have heard about the story of Joseph. The story of Joseph is the story of salvation. It's a story of hope and restoration. A story that points that God is always behind the scenes in every aspect of our lives. No matter the difficulty or what you may be going through. Or no matter how tough life is, God is with you. You may think that God hates you, or people hate you, and you start complaining, but understand that God is taking you somewhere.

God is taking you where you will be amid blessings; you will operate amid blessings. These blessings are already there. They are already worked for. Maybe they have been working for by nations or some people. They are already there for you to just receive.

Look at the story; you know what happened. Joseph's brother put him in the pit and sold him out as a slave.

So, whatever is happening with you today, if you are still with God, if you are still praying, if you are still attached with God, you will arrive at your destination. Sometimes things will be so hard, you can imagine, an Israelite becoming a slave to the Egyptians. Hallelujah, God forbid.

And so, when Jacob went to Egypt, he was a slave boy. And what can we learn from the life of Joseph? The way Joseph was tested. Joseph was tested to see whether he will still remain attached to the God of Israel and if he's God-fearing. Because, if you are in a difficult time, if you are in the time that you are down, that is your testing season to see whether you still have faith in Him, whether you will still keep His word so that the journey will continue. Unfortunately, for some people, the journey might be cut short. The journey might close because of the test. Maybe you fail the test, perhaps you cannot continue the journey. I want you to understand that there is hope in God.

The Bible says that God is not pleased with the wicked. So, the more you continue to show the fear of God, God will continue to take you through the journey, and He will help you to overcome the challenges. And that is why the Bible says that the Lord Jesus taught the disciples to pray, that let your will in heaven be done on earth exactly on how it is in heaven. If you have not yet arrived at your God-ordained destination, the journey is on, and you will get there.

So now look at the blessings of Joseph. What happened

after all that he went through? He went into prison unjustly, and finally, he became the Prime Minister in the land of Egypt. He became the spiritual father of Egypt. He was next in command to king Pharaoh, and everyone listened to him. *"And the thing was good in the eyes of Pharaoh, and in the eyes of all his servants. And Pharaoh said unto his servants, can we find such a one as this is, a man in whom the Spirit of God is? And Pharaoh said unto Joseph, Forasmuch as God hath shewed thee all this, there is none so discreet and wise as thou art: Thou shalt be over my house, and according unto thy word shall all my people be ruled: only in the throne will I be greater than thou. And Pharaoh said unto Joseph, See, I have set thee over all the land of Egypt. And Pharaoh took off his ring from his hand, and put it upon Joseph's hand, and arrayed him in vestures of fine linen, and put a gold chain about his neck; And he made him to ride in the second chariot which he had; and they cried before him, Bow the knee: and he made him ruler over all the land of Egypt. And Pharaoh said unto Joseph, I am Pharaoh, and without thee shall no man lift up his hand or foot in all the land of Egypt."*- Genesis 41:37-44

This shows that Joseph was a blessing to a nation and not just a few individuals. The blessing was for a nation, and he became a blessing to the land of Egypt. And the Egyptians, they themselves, were also happy. But that was the plan of God for the life of Joseph. Joseph was very blessed. He had everything. He was the commander of money. He was the one that was commanding money, and, he was preparing a place for his family. The family was supposed to come in the time that was supposed to come when things would be so hot, and the economy was bad.

So, God is already planning for everybody, taking care of everybody, today, tomorrow, and the days to come. So, you like that; you are so strategic and timely. As a Christian, you are placed so strategically under the blessing, a blessing to the people of God, a blessing to yourself, and a blessing to nations.

If we can go back to the story of the young girl that was attached to the story of Naaman. This young girl was a blessing to Syria because people make a nation. It is not by trees, by people. So Naaman was very important to Syria. It was because of the connection of this girl that Naaman was healed.

Let's check out another good example in the life of Esther. Esther was a girl that had lost, her parents according to scriptures. She was just staying with her uncle. So, God was using this girl, no matter the level of her spiritual maturity, God was using this girl to be a blessing for the nation of the King that he got married to, and to be a blessing and a protector to the people of God. God is always helping His people, protecting, and feeding his people by using someone.

So, you, as a Christian, God has chosen you to receive blessings and to be a blessing to His people and even to your nation. I repeat it again, God has chosen you to be a blessing of your own self in abundance and a blessing to the nation that you are residing right now, and a blessing and a protector to the family of God, to the people of God.

There are some Christians that when God have blessed them, oh, I mean that they think only about themselves and start making unnecessary comparisons with what others have that they are yet to own. God has not blessed such people. I'm more blessed than selfish people. However, when you are not opened to being a blessing, God will not be pleased because God has not made you a blessing of yourself but a blessing to his people.

So, don't ever look down on any other child of God. Never condemn them, whether they're poor or in need. Whether they are having now or don't, God has called you a blessing to the nation you are living and to yourself and His people.

These events have been repeating and repeating over and again. Hallelujah. We saw how Esther, because of her position and where she was, never knew. If you read the story of Esther, at first, she never knew that she was brought to that palace for a mission. She thought that she was so successful. She was so blessed more than other girls, and that is why she was married. She had married the King of the nation, but no, she was chosen by God for a mission.

So as Christians, we should understand that we are the agent of God. And let me say again, the agent of the glory of God, because the life of Joseph glorifies

God, so greatly. The life of Esther glorifies God so greatly. The life of the little girl that was captured in Israel to Syria glorified God so greatly. So, no matter what you may be going through, your life is destined to glorify God greatly. Your life is destined to glorify God among others. Hallelujah, hallelujah, hallelujah, hallelujah. Hallelujah.

How to Hear the Voice of God

Now let's go to the practical ways, how to hear the voice of God and how to walk with God. I began to learn how to walk with God, and I received this revelation one day. I went to eat in a restaurant, when I sat to eat, I noticed a family was sitting right in front of where I sat, and I overheard the woman saying that if she doesn't get pregnant, she would file for a divorce.

Their discussion was audible enough for me to hear. As a man who understands that he is a blessing to his generation and a problem solver, what would you suggest I do? Should I walk up to them and tell them I heard their conversation, I would like to pray with them because I believe that God can solve their marital issue?

What if God already knew they would be at that place, and He knew what they were going through and so decided to arrange that I am also in that restaurant at the same time because he knows that I would be a blessing to that couple and help them out of their crisis? So, I'll simply approach them and pray with them, and what if after three months God gives them a baby after I prayed and prophesied upon them that they would carry their baby soon

What do you think will be my recompense? These people will never forget me. These people will come to Christ. And these people will worship God because the way they talked didn't show that they were Christians. So, God permitted me to hear so that heaven can intervene in their situation through me, and God will bring about their desired change and bring salvation into their life, not just a baby into their family.

Too often, God brings such opportunities our way as His children to be a blessing to people and point them to Christ, but we squander such opportunities. We do not recognize that God is at work, and He has planned the whole event to show forth His glory in the life of some people who haven't known God. So instead, we do nothing or even make fun of their situation when we can pray for them and point them to the Messiah.

At another time, I was in transit traveling for an event when I heard a woman speaking on the phone to her husband that he will never see their children again. You will never talk to them again. Don't call me again. I don't want to hear again, your voice. Now, it seems like they were already separated. She began to scream on the telephone while I was standing there.

Then the thought came to my mind, "Why did God

bring you here, and why did God allow you to hear this conversation?" It is for your intervention. God will not come again to shout on your ears that, oh go there, because that is your training. He has taught you to know that you are a solution on the earth. You are made to solve problems, and it is only by solving these problems that God will bless you. It is not working because you work on your own. You work with your hands, work with your feet, work, and are tired. But the type of work that God will bless is the type of work that He will do through you. The work that He has planned out and ordained you to execute with Him.

So, that is why you see a lot of Christians; they go through tough times and difficulties. Most times, it is because there are a lot of opportunities that have come closer to them, and they have not taken note. They are only planning to go to church on Sunday and resume their work on Monday. They are not sensitive to God presents to them daily. They are too busy to see the opportunities that are presented to them every now and then.

Imagine if I prayed for those couples that were about to separate because of a childbearing. Imagine if I had the understanding before or had the courage to pray for them. And if it was the plan of God, this family will never forget me. And they will always live to glorify God. And they will always keep their story in honor of Jesus. So, when next you are walking in the street or a restaurant, or even in a meeting at work, always be sensitive to God's move. Always be in the Spirit and open to God's leading so that you can be available to be used as a blessing to others.

God is there with you in the restaurant. God is there with you at the train station or the airport; He is there with you in that supermarket while you are shopping. God is there, so you have to be alert because God will bring you opportunities to change your life. God will bring you opportunities to make you great. God will bring opportunities to glorify Himself when you stand to be a blessing to others.

So, for those who are working, wherever you are working, and any type of job you are doing, God has placed you there for a purpose. It is not only for the salary at the end of the month but there is something bigger than the salary that God has planned for you to achieve one day. So, you must always be praying for God not to miss that one day. That is the day that God has planned for you to become a millionaire. One day, God has planned for you to change your life. We all have that one day in our life, the day for you to become huge and become great.

Remember we talked about the little girl captured in Israel and taken to Syria; when that day arrived, that girl acted in line with the divine plan, and I'm sure she was handsomely rewarded by Naaman when he returned clean healed. Also, remember the story of Joseph? When that day arrived, Joseph was called from prison, and Joseph acted well in line with divine purpose, and he also became great. Remember the story of Esther that we had talked about when the day arrived for her as well; she was sensitive. Esther knew that day for a longer time because Esther was fasting and praying before the day. You know, some people have the advantage of knowing the day ahead.

So, for those working, whether as an entrepreneur or an independent consultant, whether you are working for somebody, whichever work you do, that day is here. That day is coming. It is that day that I have come to inform you. The day that God has already ordained to make you great. Don't miss that day.

Everyone has that day. It is from that day that you start to flow in prosperity. The day that God will use you to bring glory to His name among men. It is that day that the Lord will use you to bless people, bless his people, and bless even the nations. I want you to believe that you are ordained as a blessing.

Let me share this striking experience with you. I applied for a job in a company, and I was invited for an interview. After the interview, I was selected. So, in that company, you have to see the director-general. So, I climbed upstairs to meet with the person after I had signed all the documents. Although the purpose for visiting the director-general was to have a handshake and welcome to the company.

So, when I got to his office, the director-general was

on the phone. So, I sat there, and where I was, I could hear his conversation on the phone. The man was complaining on the phone about his eyes, that his eyes were getting dimmer and dimmer every day. He said he had seen the best doctors and even consultants have checked his eyes. He said he had spent a lot and in fact, he had to spend about 150 euros on seeing a consultant. But all to no avail. His eyes were not getting better but growing worse.

After he concluded his conversation on the phone, he came to attend to me; then, I got the courage to talk to him, laying aside my purpose for coming to see him. I said, "Mr. Director, I heard what you were saying on the phone regarding your eyes and how all your efforts seem to be in futility. But no matter what you are going through, I know somebody that can help you."

"I continued that if you believe in Jesus Christ, He will heal you now and hear immediately." That was what I said in the office. Now, the director said that, so you are a believer. I said yes, I'm a believer. The director didn't accept that I should pray for him because it might not be the plan of God. So, you might be doing this, and nothing happens. It does not mean that any of the events God has planned it. The events that God has already planned and ordained will always work out. So don't give up or be discouraged. Don't be annoyed or blame yourself that you have missed it. No, you have not missed it because the one that God has planned and ordained is coming.

So, continue. Even if you want to pray for somebody and the person refuses, there is no problem with that. But keep on the courage and being available to help people, especially in that case. Just imagine if God ordained for me to pray for the director, and he agreed, and God healed him, hallelujah. A director of that type of company, I don't know what he would have done to me; that man would take me to his spiritual advisor. I will be a spiritual advisor of that company. I will just have my own office there. And I don't know what he could have done for me, but it could have been something great because the man was really, really suffering from those eyes problem.

Imagine a man holding a prominent position in a multimillion-dollar company, and his eyes are going dim. The man would be blind, and you from nowhere, and brought a solution to that man. I don't want to guess, but that man would bless you. The man would do you good. Those are the things God has planned and ordained to help His own people.

The problem is that you might be listening to a man like that caliber, but you don't have the courage to pray. You don't have the faith to pray for the person. You can refer the man to a pastor. Also, if the pastor prays for the man and the man gets healed, you too will be blessed because you are the bridge for the solution of the man. Exactly, like the girl who was kidnapped from Israel to Syria. The girl didn't pray for Naaman, but the girl referred Naaman to the prophet.

So, you always have a part to play; either you execute the action or refer the person to somebody, you will always be part of it.

Another example that I'd like to share is the spiritual dimension of being a blessing. There is also a physical part that you should always be helpful to those in need. For example, you can be moving, and you see somebody crying that oh I have missed my flight, or I've missed my train and I don't have any other money, because I bought the ticket with the last money, I had on me. I don't even have money to stay for one night in a hotel or even buy another ticket as my ticket is nonrefundable.

So, what would you do in that case? If God placed that type of situation in front of you, God would be looking at you if you had the understanding that you are a blessing. If that type of case presents itself, if it was the will of God, you will have exactly the amount needed to bring joy to such an already devastated soul.

I once had a case like that. I had the exact amount that the person needed. Truth is, God cannot put you into situations that you are uncomfortable with, God cannot bring you somebody to you with a financial problem, and you don't have the money to fix their issue. If it is God's plan, God will bring you a situation that He knows the amount of money you have in your pocket is enough to glorify Him before that person in need. God will bring that person knowing that you have the understanding to solve that problem.

So, you see, those are the things that you have to do to enter and obtain the blessing of God. Remember God has ordained a day to make you great. There is a day that God has ordained to make you become a millionaire. There is a day that God has ordained to make you rich. There is a day that God has ordained, don't miss that.

So out of all this, I understand that you have understood why you became a Christian. You have become a Christian to be somebody great, but you must have the understanding at any moment that you have an opportunity, and you see people begging, even if you don't have enough money to take care of them, you have to always pray for them. Pray for them in your heart. Pray sincerely for the power of God, for the revelation of God, to fall upon them. It means that you are alert. You are always alert. You are always waiting, and you are always expecting that God will do the supernatural in their lives.

God told Abraham in Genesis 12:2-3, *"And I will make of thee a great nation, and I will bless thee, and make thy name great; and thou shalt be a blessing: And I will bless them that bless thee, and curse him that curseth thee: and in thee shall all families of the earth be blessed."* God's plan for Abraham was to bless him and make him a blessing.

You may be thinking, "Well, that's Abraham, not me." See what God said in Isaiah 51:2, *"Look unto Abraham your father, and unto Sarah that bare you: for I called him alone, and blessed him, and increased him."* In other words, study the life of Abraham and see my plan for his life. See how I made him a blessing to many. That is what I will do to you also. Abraham was rich in silver and gold, and he had over three hundred servants born in his house.

So, stop seeking to be blessed alone. Stop thinking and praying about yourself alone. God has ordained to make you a man of wealth, so get set to be a blessing also. Open your heart and trust God not to miss that day He has planned.

CHAPTER 4

WRAPPED IN THE WORD

It's no longer news that God has a colorful plan for you and that He is mindful of you. You are His priority, and your wellbeing is of utmost importance to Him. But you may ask, "So where can I find God's plan for my life?" "How do I know God's plan for my life?"

God's plans for your life are detailed throughout the Bible; It is wrapped up in the word. The Bible is a compilation of God's mind for you and what He has ordained for you from the foundation of the earth. All of God's promises in scriptures point to you and refer to you just like a parcel bearing your name and address.

Now, you may ask, "Is it right for me to take promises given to the people of Israel or Moses or David, or the disciples and apply them to my life today?" "Can I just take what God said to Abraham and then assume it is His plan for my life as well?" "I wasn't there when Jesus was preaching; how can I conclude that what He was saying also talks about me?" "I wasn't a member of the churches that Apostle Paul and the other Apostles wrote letters to; how can you say the Bible contains God's plan for me?" Basically, the answer is an emphatic "Yes!" Let me show you why this is so.

First, the Bible says in 2 Corinthians 1:20, *"For all the promises of God in Him are Yes, and in Him Amen, to the glory of God through us."* All of God's Words are yes and set to be fulfilled without exceptions. Also, Jesus said in Mark 13:37, *"And what I say to you, I say to all."* In other words, what God said to them in the Bible days wasn't just for them, He was, and He is saying to us also today. His promises to them are also relevant to you today. His plan to proper them and heal them is still in force in your life today.

You see, not only is Jesus the ultimate fulfilment of all the promises, but He is the key to the promises. So, when we are in Christ, we are entitled to the same blessing and provision of scriptures. In Christ, we receive the promises and can call them ours; we see His plan and call them ours. Why? They are in the canon of scripture and part of Christ's inheritance through His finished work on the Cross of Calvary.

Now check out these verses in Galatians 3:13-14, 29, *"Christ has redeemed us from the curse of the law, having become a curse for us (for it is written, "Cursed is everyone who hangs on a tree"), 14 that the blessing of Abraham might come upon the Gentiles in Christ Jesus, that we might receive the promise of the Spirit through faith... And if you are Christ's, then you are Abraham's seed, and heirs according to the promise."* Did you catch that truth?

Once you are in Christ, you are an heir of the Father

and entitled to Abrahamic blessings, which is passed down to his seed, Isaac, and to you. The Bible says in Galatians 4:28, *"Now we, brethren, as Isaac was, are the children of promise."* Christ is the divine connection that connects you to the promises of God and enlists you as one of those that God has ordained to enrich. So, despite your race, colour, language, background, status, or gender, I want you to know one thing for sure that you qualify. Isn't that amazing?

You see, God has plans for nations, for people or a group, and for individuals. The book of Isaiah 46:10–11 summarizes what God wants us to know about His plans: *"My purpose will stand, and I will do all that I please. From the east, I summon a bird of prey; from a far-off land, a man to fulfill my purpose. What I have said that I will bring about; what I have planned, that I will do."* It's one thing to recognize that God has an overarching plan for the world; it is quite another to acknowledge that God has a specific plan for each person.

Yes, it's easy to assume that God's word contains His plan for your church or the nation but as true as that is, I want you to believe today that He has a specific plan for your life. The Bible says in Luke 12:7, *"But even the very hairs of your head are all numbered."* In other words, God has enough time not just to count the hair of your hair, but He meticulously numbered them. Do you know what that means? He is particular about you, and He has great plans for you.

Many places in scripture indicate that God does

have a specific plan for each human being. It starts before we were conceived in the womb. The Lord told Jeremiah, *"Before I formed you in the womb I knew you, before you were born I set you apart; I appointed you as a prophet to the nations"* (Jeremiah 1:5). God's plan was not reactive or a response to Jeremiah's conception. It was preemptive, implying God specially formed this male child to accomplish His plan. David underscores this truth: *"You created my inmost being; you knit me together in my mother's womb"* (Psalm 139:13).

Unborn children are not accidents. They are formed in the womb by the Creator for His purposes and to fulfill His plan. That is one reason abortion is wrong. We have no right to disrespect God's plan and violate God's workmanship by killing a child He is in the process of forming. Once God forms a child in a womb, a dimension of His plan is set in motion, and He begins to watch it. But when the pregnancy is aborted, the plan is aborted, and God's purpose is truncated.

God's plan for every human being is that each one comes to know Him and accept His offer of salvation. The Bible says in 2 Peter 3:9, *"The Lord is not slack concerning his promise, as some men count slackness; but is longsuffering to us-ward, not willing that any should perish, but that all should come to repentance."*

He created us for fellowship with Him, and, when we reject the reconciliation He offers, we live at cross purposes with His plan for us. Salvation is the foundation on which we partake of God's plan for our lives. The Bible says in John 3:16, *"For God so loved the world, that he gave his only begotten Son, that whosoever believeth in him should not perish, but have everlasting life."* This scripture is the ultimate plan of God for all humanity. He desired that all men be saved and God to the knowledge of the truth.

However, God also designed good works for us according to our gifts, strengths, and opportunities beyond salvation. His word said in Ephesians 2:10, *"For we are his workmanship, created in Christ Jesus unto good works, which God hath before ordained that we should walk in them."*

He orchestrated the location and time into which each of us is born. You weren't born in that country and into that family accidentally. He knew why you should be born in that location, and at the time you were born. It's all part of His plan, and your life is simply a playback of His design and His chosen. Psalm 139:16, *"But with your own eyes you saw my body being formed. Even before I was born, you had written in your book everything I would do. Your thoughts are far beyond my understanding, much more than I could ever imagine."*

If He knows the number of hairs on our heads, then He knows us better than we know ourselves. He knows our gifts, talents, strengths, and weaknesses. And He knows how we could best use them to make an eternal impact. The Bible says in 1 Corinthians

12:7-11, *"The Spirit has given each of us a special way of serving others. Some of us can speak with wisdom, while others can speak with knowledge, but these gifts come from the same Spirit. To others, the Spirit has given great faith or the power to heal the sick. Or the power to work mighty miracles. Some of us are prophets, and some of us recognize when God's Spirit is present. Others can speak different kinds of languages, and still others can tell what these languages mean. But it is the Spirit who does all this and decides which gifts to give to each of us."* He gave us different gifts and talents according to our special abilities. Through the Spirit of God, we are given various abilities and spiritual strengths to serve His purpose on the earth. So, nothing about our lives is a waste.

Also, God gives us opportunities to store up treasures in heaven so that, for all eternity, we can enjoy His reward. Matthew 10:41–42 says, *"Anyone who welcomes a prophet, just because that person is a prophet, will be given the same reward as a prophet. Anyone who welcomes a good person, just because that person is good, will be given the same reward as a good person. And anyone who gives one of my most humble followers a cup of cool water, just because that person is my follower, will surely be rewarded."*

God's plan for each person is generally stated in Micah 6:8: *"He has told you, O man, what is good; and what does the LORD require of you but to do justice, and to love kindness, and to walk humbly with your God?"* His plan is for relationships over duties. When we walk in the Spirit (Galatians 5:16, 25), enjoying a loving relationship with the Lord, our actions indicate that closeness. Pleasing Him is our delight. His plan unfolds naturally as we grow in faith, mature in knowledge, and practice obedience with all we understand. As we obey His general plan for His children, we discover His uniquely designed plan for our lives.

Therefore, it's time to embrace God's word, which contains his design and plan for your life. His ultimate purpose for all humanity is wrapped up in His word and particularly for you as an individual. So, always see everything from the lens of scripture. Do well to interpret the events of your life as a fulfillment of God's purpose. You are not a mistake. You are a deliberate creation of God.

CHAPTER 5

YOU ARE STILL ON TRACK

As children of God, part of God's plan is for us to reach out to others with the good news of salvation. Jesus' last statement before His final ascension to heaven is in Matthew 28:19-29, which says, *"Go to the people of all nations and make them my disciples. Baptize them in the name of the Father, the Son, and the Holy Spirit, and teach them to do everything I have told you. I will be with you always, even until the end of the world."* He commissions us to fulfill His purpose, which is turning many to righteousness. Our lives and conducts must be a worthy example that draws many to Christ.

His plan is clearly stated in 2 Corinthians 5:19-20, which says, *"To wit, that God was in Christ, reconciling the world unto himself, not imputing their trespasses unto them; and hath committed unto us the word of reconciliation. Now then we are ambassadors for Christ, as though God did beseech you by us: we pray you in Christ's stead, be ye reconciled to God."* In other words, Jesus came to reconcile us back to God, and when He left, He handed over the baton of reconciliation to us. You should preach the Gospel with your life and verbally tell people about the love of Christ.

Apostle Paul understood this divine purpose. He said

in 1 Corinthians 9:16, *"For though I preach the gospel, I have nothing to glory of: for necessity is laid upon me; yea, woe is unto me, if I preach not the gospel!"* He placed His life under compulsion to always preach the Gospel and turn many to Christ. Now let me show you one more reason you should live to fulfill this divine plan. Now check out this verse in 2 Corinthians 5:11, *"Knowing therefore the terror of the Lord, we persuade men; but we are made manifest unto God; and I trust also are made manifest in your consciences."* If you understand the judgment that awaits anyone that does not accept the free offer of salvation, you will make haste to compel them and pray for their salvation.

Friend, you need to start fulfilling that divine purpose by preaching to your family member or parents, or colleagues who are yet to accept Jesus. To show how passionate you are about God's plan for your life, you may have to mention their names in prayer for God to save them.

Also, His plan is for His children to conform to the likeness of Jesus Christ. The Bible says in Romans 8:29, *"For whom he did foreknow, he also did predestinate to be conformed to the image of his Son, that he might be the firstborn among many brethren."* God ordained you to be like Christ in morals and conduct. The bible also commands in *Romans* 12:2, *"And be not conformed to this world: but be ye transformed by the renewing of your mind, that ye may prove what is that good, and acceptable, and perfect, will of God."* His plan for you is that the nature of Christ swallows up your nature.

This implies that your behavior is not based on your environment or influence by peer pressure or financial or economic demands, but by the word of God. Conforming to Christ means to pattern your life after the word of God. He wants us to grow in grace and knowledge of the truth of scriptures. (2 Peter 3:18). He wants us to love other Christians the way He loves us (John 13:34).

As we follow His Word, we will discover our spiritual gifts and abilities that specially suit us to serve Him in unique ways. God's plan unfolds in our lives as we use all we have for His glory. Paul admonishes us in 1 Corinthians 10:31, *"Whether therefore ye eat, or drink, or whatsoever ye do, do all to the glory of God."*

However, we often become impatient in wondering what God's plan is for our lives. But it is not as complicated as we make it out to be. God's plan for us is revealed little by little and not as sudden as we always think.

For instance, when the children of Israel left Egypt, God's plan for them is to possess the land of their enemies. He said to them in Exodus 23:29-30, *"I will not drive them out from before thee in one year; lest the land become desolate, and the beast of the field multiply against thee. By little and little I will drive them out from before thee, until thou be increased, and inherit the land."* In other words, His plan for them will unfold gradually. He will drive their enemies out of the land one at a time. That's how he does for us even today.

Some people want to have a luxurious car, build mansions, own properties, become CEO of a large organization, and have billions of dollars in their account before their twenty-first birthday. Don't get me wrong, this is possible and God's desire for you. But sometimes situations may not line up as you expect. God may give you a car and then prepare you until later before giving you the office space. It's all God's plan. So, patience is a necessary virtue if we must walk and live in God's ordained plan for our lives.

On the other hand, as we follow Him, His plan may look different in different seasons of our life. We may even start to question if we are in God's plan for not.

For instance, a young woman may ask God to direct her to His plan and believes college is part of that plan. But halfway through college, she falls ill and must spend the next two years in a convalescent home. Is she now out of God's plan? Not if her heart is set to obey Him. In that convalescent home, she meets a young man who becomes her husband. They both love the Lord and desire to serve Him and believe that His plan for them is the mission field. They begin preparation, but she becomes pregnant with a high-risk pregnancy halfway through the training. Did they miss God's plan? Has the Lord abandoned them? Not at all.

Because of their experience caring for a child with special needs, they can minister to other families with similar needs. Their mission field looks much different from their envisioned one, but it is God's plan for them. They are able to look back and see His hand in every turn along the way.

Does this sound like your story? Is your life rolling in cycles, and you wonder if you are still in step with His divine plan? Perhaps things aren't falling in line as you want to, and you aren't sure if God is still in your favor? I want you to know that God still loves you, and nothing can change that truth. You are His delight, and He knows how to turn things around for your good.

Do you remember the story of Ruth in the scriptures? She was a Moabite whose tribe was cursed and weren't supposed to ever appear in the assembly of God's people. But God had a plan for this precious lady. By divine plan, she got married to the sons of Elimelech, a Benjaminite. The family relocated to Moab to seek a better life because of famine.

After a while, her husband died before she had any child, and now her mother-in-law is miserable. She has lost her husband and her children in the land of the Moabites. Ruth's life looks like it has just been placed in reversed gear. The question would be, is Ruth still aligned with God's plan?

Soon her mother-in-law, Naomi, planned to return

home from Moab, and Ruth decided to follow her. When they got back while trying to take care of Naomi, Ruth met a wealthy man, named Boaz who was from the same family as her late husband, and they eventually got married. They gave birth to a son named Obed, who became the father of Jesse and the grandfather of King David. In other words, through her marriage to Boaz, Ruth became enlisted to the linage of Jesus. Isn't that amazing?

Her life looks like it was moving on a downward slope, but God was part of the story. These stories should encourage you also. No matter what you are facing, it's all part of God's plan. He has a plan to bring you into the fullness of His purpose for your life. His plan is to enrich you and make you a person of influence. So, take a back seat and trust God. Trust His ability to turn all things around for your good. It's all part of God's plan

CHAPTER 6

THE PILGRIM'S PROGRESS

Life can sometimes be described as a journey. Interestingly, each of us has a unique path that we must follow as we voyage through the bend and freeway of life until we arrive at our desired destination. Like an Uber taxi driver, who terminates a trip as a passenger highlight from the vehicle and starts another trip for the next passenger, so is the journey of life. Our arrival at a destination flags off the commencement of another journey with a defined and unique destination.

Too often, we all wish the journey can be like a freeway without speed breakers or U-turn. For instance, we all want to grow up, get to high school, and then to the University of our choice, graduate, get a high paying job that makes you afford the best of life, marry your desired spouse, give birth to lovely kids, and then live happily ever after. As sweet as this sounds, the journey of life is never designed to flow in this manner.

Like life's journey, God's plan for your life is rarely a straight shot to a visible goal. His plan requires of us a journey, illustrated so well in Bunyan's "The Pilgrim's Progress," and that journey may be filled with detours, sudden stops, and confusing turns. But the good news is that the destination is sure. Jesus had a long discussion with His disciples towards His last moments on the earth. In John 16:33, He said, *"These things I have spoken unto you, that in me ye might have peace. In the world ye shall have tribulation: but be of good cheer; I have overcome the world."*

This statement showed a portion of their journey after He was gone. They have had an awesome time with Him going from one crusade to another, traveling from one city to another. They have witnessed the mighty move of God demonstrated by Jesus, while they have also demonstrated a few dimensions of God's power. Remember their testimony in Luke 10:17, *"And the seventy returned again with joy, saying, Lord, even the devils are subject unto us through thy name."* This was one of the exploits they commanded when Jesus was with them.

Now, it was time to return home, and Jesus told them point-blank that they shouldn't think it would be business as usual. As they plan to fulfill God's plan, they will face tribulations, there will be times of persecution, but in the end, they will overcome. That is the word of God to you also.

Now, let share a glimpse of *The Pilgrim's Progress* with you as it relates to our journey on the earth. It begins with a Christian man who found the conviction to change his way and embark on a journey to the Celestial City. He knew the path to follow, and at the beginning, it looks as though the journey will be seamless, safe, and fast. His destination was promising, and the beautiful sight of the Celestial City was all that matters in Christian's mind. In fact, he was willing to leave his family behind rather than stay back and abort the journey. Unknown to him, there will be more in the way than what he bargained for.

Christian's goal was to find a place of refuge, a place of pure joy, for him and his family. However, in a moment of hopelessness, Christian meets a man called Evangelist, who points the way to his desired destination, which sounds like a good step in the right direction.

However, on his journey, Christian encounters numerous obstacles such that some individuals even attempt to convince him to abort the journey and return home. But despite the distractions, doubt, and discouragements, he went on. Along the way, Christian got to Mount Calvary, where he dropped off every weight slowing him down.

He was later given a scroll, a suit of armor, and a two-edged sword (which is the Bible). With these, he overcame all oppositions on his path like Apollyon, and he also survived a horrifying walk through the Valley of the Shadow of Death by reciting Psalm 23, which says, *"Yea, though I walk through the valley of the shadow of death, I will fear no evil: for thou art with; thy rod and thy staff they comfort me"*

He joined with a man named Faithful, and both of them faced further opposition and harassment. In the process, they were imprisoned and, when they later escaped, they continued on the journey as a team. Along the way, their faith was put to the test. They were harassed and ridiculed by the people of Vanity. Their reluctance to buy any of the material items being peddled by the shopkeepers at the fair leads to a trial. At this point in the story, Faithful is executed while Christian was saved by Hopeful, a resident of Vanity. The two would then continue to the Celestial City together. Their journey would prove no easier moving forward as they encounter Giant Despair, who captures from the dungeon; they both crossed the river of Death and were joyously welcomed to the Celestial City.

Just as Christian arrived at His destination, my prayer for you is that you will arrive at your destination as well. So long you stick to God's plan for your life and seek to obey Him. There may be opposition; some people will even advise you to turn; others will advise you to refrain from following God's plan for your life because the pain is not worth it. They may offer a cheap alternative to a destination which most definitely can't be your *Celestial City* but some other places. But you need to hang in there. If your wealthy future is not real, God wouldn't have told you about it. He is called the Alpha and Omega. The Bible says in Hebrews 10:23, *"Let us hold fast the profession of our faith without wavering; for he is faithful that promised;"*

I came across the story of Kenneth Erwin Hagin, an

American preacher who was known for pioneering the Word of Faith movement. If you've read his books on faith or listened to his sermon, you may as well think he fell from heaven and was a preacher from the womb. Well, let me burst your bubbles; this Great man of God never had a smooth journey while growing up. In fact, one would wonder how he survived and where he contacted the strength to meet up with the demands of ministry at his level and in his days.

When Kenneth clocked fifteen years old, he began to fall sick till he became bedridden. His early birth deformity had finally caught up with him. The doctor could link his illness with his deformed heart, which was earlier detected at his birth. They told his parents that Kenneth had gotten to the end of the road. Now, there was no other way but the chasm of death. Even though the baby had survived the battle for his life when he was born with a severe medical condition, the boy was now going to die as the doctor could no longer guarantee any positive medical procedure.

Eventually, Kenneth Hagin laid on what was meant to be his death bed in one of the rooms at his grandpa's house. While his grandma, mother, and younger brother sat next to him. Most of the family members were already giving up on the helpless young boy, but his mother did not. She prayed and interceded on his behalf, and God heard her. To everyone's amazement, Kenneth woke back to life in his grandma's hands while his mother was praying for him. Her undying love and compassion for her baby pushed her to pray for him, and she didn't stop until he was healed. From that moment, everything turned. He went on to fulfil God's plan for his life by been blessing many even after his call to eternal glory.

For instance, look at the life of Moses in the scriptures. God's ultimate plan for this humble man is to lead over three million Israelites out of slavery in Egypt into the land God has promised their father. A land flowing with milk and honey. Sounds good, right? So, the journey should be like, Moses is born, raised, and like Samuel, finds His way to the temple, and then one day, he leads the people out of the front gate of Egypt while Pharaoh and all their masters watch them go. That's a cool journey, isn't it? Even Moses wished it was that straight.

Now, don't get me wrong, I am not advocating evil, struggle, or hardship. No matter what you face; they are all part of God's plan to lead you to your destination.

Baby Moses was born at a time when there was a decree by Pharaoh to kill all the male children born among the Israelites. Exodus 1:22 (ERV), *"So Pharaoh gave this command to his own people: 'If the Hebrew women give birth to a baby girl, let it live. But if they have a baby boy, you must throw it into the Nile River."* It was as though God's plan will be truncated and will not see the light of the day. Medical science will put it this way, "dead on arrival."

Well, the boy escaped the sentence through a slight margin of death when his mother decided to let go and placed him at the bank of the river. But God has a better. He orchestrated Moses' return to his mother, who took care of Him, and Pharaoh's daughter paid her.

Moses grew to become a Prince in Egypt, but he always knew that flaunting Egypt's wealth and prestige was not all that God had ordained for Him. For forty years, he was a prince in Egypt, and he learned the ways and culture of the Egyptians. He expected that they already knew God's plan for his life, and he felt since he already had the influence, he could simply negotiate their freedom. But an attempt to reveal His purpose when he was forty years took him straight to the bush, and the prince became a fugitive.

For the next forty years, his life looks like it was at a standstill until he encountered God at the age of eighty, and then he was back on track with divine purpose, leading the people of God out of Egypt.

You see, no matter the challenges, you will surely get to your destination. Therefore, set your hearts to obey God in all that you do, then you will remain in the center of His will every step of the way. Obedience is a capital virtue for anyone that will go through the pilgrimage of life and manifest God's ordained plan for them. What has God told you? Where has He told you to go to? What are the things He has commanded you to stop doing? What are the steps that you were told to take?

Remember, God's plans are not revealed in bulk but in bits. And as we obey, the next phase of His plan opens up. So, keep obeying God, and His ordained plan will be opened to you.

CHAPTER 7

DECRYPTING GOD'S VOICE

Now that you are set to obey God, I think the next question you will probably ask is, "How can we recognize the voice of God?" Understand that the voice of God is a vital asset in discovering and maximizing God's plan for your life. Many great men in scriptures that ever walked with God had access to the voice of God.

Why is the voice of the Lord important? Remember, I shared in the previous chapter that life is a journey, and fulfilling His plan is the destination. But how can you navigate a terrain you are not used to? How can you travel on an unknown path without guidance? Too often, many promising and vibrant believers fade off because they only got a go-ahead from God but failed to stay on with the voice of God as a compass to direct their way through the adventure of life.

See what the Psalmist said about the voice of God:

"The voice of the LORD is upon the waters: the God of glory thundereth: the LORD is upon many waters. The voice of the LORD is powerful; the voice of the LORD is full of majesty. The voice of the LORD breaketh the cedars; yea, the LORD breaketh the cedars of Lebanon. He maketh them also to skip like a calf; Lebanon and Sirion like a young unicorn. The

voice of the LORD divideth the flames of fire. The voice of the LORD shaketh the wilderness; the LORD shaketh the wilderness of Kadesh. The voice of the LORD maketh the hinds to calve, and discovereth the forests: and in his temple doth every one speak of his glory." – Psalm 29:3-9

So, recognizing God's voice is critical in your walk with God. Let me show you some examples of men that couldn't operate in the fullness of God's plan for their life until they learned to recognize the voice of God.

The Bible talks about a young man named Samuel who heard the voice of God but did not recognize it until he was instructed by his leader, Eli.

"And the child Samuel ministered unto the LORD before Eli. And the word of the LORD was precious in those days; there was no open vision. And it came to pass at that time, when Eli was laid down in his place, and his eyes began to wax dim, that he could not see; And ere the lamp of God went out in the temple of the LORD, where the ark of God was, and Samuel was laid down to sleep; That the LORD called Samuel: and he answered, Here am I. And he ran unto Eli, and said, Here am I; for thou calledst me. And he said, I called not; lie down again. And he went and lay down. And the LORD called yet again, Samuel. And Samuel arose and went to Eli, and said, Here am I; for thou didst call me. And he answered, I called not, my son; lie down again. Now Samuel did not yet know the LORD, neither was the word of the LORD yet revealed unto him. And the LORD called Samuel again the third time. And he arose and went to Eli, and said, Here am I; for thou

didst call me. And Eli perceived that the LORD had called the child. Therefore Eli said unto Samuel, Go, lie down: and it shall be, if he call thee, that thou shalt say, Speak, LORD; for thy servant heareth. So Samuel went and lay down in his place. And the LORD came, and stood, and called as at other times, Samuel, Samuel. Then Samuel answered, Speak; for thy servant heareth." – 1 Samuel 3:1–10

Samuel had lived and served in the temple for a while but still couldn't recognize God's voice when it was directed to Him. He knew how to prepare the altar for sacrifice, he knew how to clean the vessel, and in fact, he was responsible for opening the temple every morning. Yet, he didn't know how to recognize God's voice until Prophet Eli guided him.

Also, did you observe that Samuel didn't have a clue about God's ultimate plan for his life regarding leading the nation of Israel and taking over from Eli until he was able to recognize God's voice? His voice is pertinent if you must maximize His purpose and plan for your life.

Also, let's check out another hero of faith who couldn't recognizes God's voice at some point in his life. Gideon had a physical revelation from God, and he still doubted what he had heard to the point of asking for a sign, not once, but three times.

Let's see Judges 6:17-20, *"And he said unto him, If now I have found grace in thy sight, then shew me a sign that thou talkest with me. Depart not hence, I pray thee, until I come unto thee, and bring forth my present, and set it before thee. And he said, I will tarry until thou come again. And Gideon went in, and made ready a kid, and unleavened cakes of an ephah of flour: the flesh he put in a basket, and he put the broth in a pot, and brought it out unto him under the oak, and presented it. And the angel of God said unto him, Take the flesh and the unleavened cakes, and lay them upon this rock, and pour out the broth. And he did so."*

Gideon had a face-to-face conversation with the Lord, yet he couldn't decrypt his voice. He kept asking questions and seeking affirmations about God's plan for his life and for the deliverance of God's people from the slavery of the Midianites.

Saul, who later became Apostle Paul, is another example in the New Testament of a man who couldn't recognize God's voice when He spoke to him on his way to Damascus.

"And as he journeyed, he came near Damascus: and suddenly there shined round about him a light from heaven: And he fell to the earth, and heard a voice saying unto him, Saul, Saul, why persecuteth thou me? And he said, Who art thou, Lord? And the Lord said, I am Jesus whom thou persecuteth: it is hard for thee to kick against the pricks."

So, you need a desperate desire to recognize God's voice so you can have a comprehensive grasp of His plan for your life.

Now, you may ask, when we listen to God's voice, how can we know that He is the one speaking?

First, understand that we are a blessed generation. I said so because we do not have a similar limitation that Samuel and Gideon had; we have something they didn't readily have access to, which is the word of God. We have the complete Bible, the inspired Word of God, to read, study, and meditate on.

The Bible says in 2 Timothy 3:16–17, *"All Scripture is God-breathed and is useful for teaching, rebuking, correcting and training in righteousness, so that the man of God may be thoroughly equipped for every good work."* When we have a question about a specific topic or decision in our lives, we should see what the Bible says about it. God will never lead us contrary to what He has taught in His Word. Titus 1:2 says, *"In hope of eternal life, which God, that cannot lie, promised before the world began;"*

The Bible is the voice of God in printed form. It is not just an encyclopedia of religious words but the direct words of God. See how Apostle Peter describes the word of God.

"For we have not followed cunningly devised fables, when we made known unto you the power and coming of our Lord Jesus Christ, but were eyewitnesses of his majesty. For he received from God the Father honour and glory, when there came such a voice to him from the excellent glory, This is my beloved Son, in whom I am well pleased. And this voice which came from heaven we heard, when we were with him in the holy mount. We have also a more sure word of prophecy; whereunto ye do well that ye take heed, as unto a light that shineth in a dark place, until the day dawn, and the day star arise in your hearts: Knowing

this first, that no prophecy of the scripture is of any private interpretation. For the prophecy came not in old time by the will of man: but holy men of God spake as they were moved by the Holy Ghost."- 2 Peter 1:16-21

In other words, Peter was saying that although he was a first-hand eyewitness to the person of Christ and the gospel, the Bible is still the final say that validates their testimonies about Christ. God is the author and the chief editor of the Bible. David said in Psalm 68:11, *"The Lord gave the word: great was the company of those that published it."* Did you catch that? God gave the word to those that published it. Why? So, the Bible in your hand, or on your desk, or the e-format on your cell phone or tablets is the voice of God transcribed by Holy men.

I think you need to start appreciating what you have. Believe me; it's your most priceless possession, regardless of how much property you have acquired. So, with the Bible, you have access to the voice of God and access to the plan of God for your life. Halleluyah!

Codes for God's Voice

You may ask, "But I have the Bible, and I read it regularly, yet I don't have access to God's voice." Yes, you may be right because God's voice is not accessible by anyone who can read the Bible's letterings. There are specific spiritual requirements before you can maximize the voice of God from the scriptures. Let me share some of them as a litmus test to check where you are missing it and quickly make amends.

1. You must belong to God; you must be born again.

Jesus said, *"My sheep listen to my voice; I know them, and they follow me."* John 10:27. Those who hear God's voice are those who belong to Him—those who His grace has saved through faith in the Lord Jesus. These are the sheep who hear and recognize His voice because they know Him as their Shepherd. If you are to recognize God's voice, then you must belong to Him.

Jesus said to His disciples in John 15:15, *"Henceforth I call you not servants; for the servant knoweth not what his lord doeth: but I have called you friends; for all things that I have heard of my Father I have made known unto you."* That is, they now have access to the voice of God because they now belong to Christ. They aren't strangers anymore; they are now members of the family. Jesus usually speaks in parables before the Pharisees while He took His time to interpret to His disciples. Why? Mark 4:10-12, *"And when he was alone, they that were about him with the twelve asked of him the parable. And he said unto them, Unto you it is given to know the mystery of the kingdom of God: but unto them that are without, all these things are done in parables: That seeing they may see, and not perceive; and hearing they may hear, and not understand; lest at any time they should be converted, and their sins should be forgiven them."*

So, are you saved? Have you repented of your sin and confessed Jesus as your Lord and personal savior? Have you renounced the devil and his works in your life and embraced the finished work of Christ on Calvary? If not, you need to pause this book and take that step by faith. Confess your sin and ask Jesus to forgive you. On the contrary, if you are saved, let's check out other codes to decrypt God's voice.

2. Spend time in Bible study and quiet contemplation of His Word.

When your child hears your voice often, even when you are near but not close to the child, he would know that's you. The same applies to our relationship with God. The more time we spend intimately with God and His Word, the easier it is to recognize His voice and His leading in our lives. For instance, employees at a bank are trained to recognize counterfeits by studying genuine money so closely that it is easy to spot a fake at a glance.

So, we should be so familiar with God's Word that when someone speaks error to us, it is clear that it is not of God. While God could speak audibly to people today, He speaks primarily through His written Word. David said in Psalm 119:97-98, *"O how love I thy law! It is my meditation all day. Thou through thy commandments hast made me wiser than mine enemies: for they are ever with me."* He was a man so passionate about the voice of God that he studied the Bible, on several occasions when he needed to know God's plan for his life, and he had to inquire from God. Also, he said in Psalm 119:11, *"Thy word have I hid in mine heart, that I might not sin against thee."* In other words, through your word, I have access to your voice that guides me from errors and making mistakes. Have a time alone with the Bible so you can hear the voice of God and understand to what extent He has ordained you to be rich.

3. Through the Holy Spirit.

Next to salvation is to seek the baptism of the Holy Spirit. Now check out this passage in Act 19:1-6, *"And it came to pass, that, while Apollos was at Corinth, Paul having passed through the upper coasts came to Ephesus: and finding certain disciples, He said unto them, Have ye received the Holy Ghost since ye believed? And they said unto him, We have not so much as heard whether there be any Holy Ghost. And he said unto them, Unto what then were ye baptized? And they said, Unto John's baptism. Then said Paul, John verily baptized with the baptism of repentance, saying unto the people, that they should believe on him which should come after him, that is, on Christ Jesus. When they heard this, they were baptized in the name of the Lord Jesus. And when Paul had laid his hands upon them, the Holy Ghost came on them; and they spake with tongues, and prophesied."*

Paul had to confirm if they were baptized in the Holy Spirit because he knew they had a glorious destiny, and they may not access God's plan except they are filled with the Holy Spirit. You see, God is Spirit, and it takes tuning to the Spirit to decode what He is saying per time. Jesus told the disciples that the Holy

Spirit would teach them all things. So, when you are filled with the Holy Spirit, it's always a spirit-to-spirit communication. Praise God. So, take that step now.

4. Through our consciences.

James H. Aughey once said, *"Conscience is the voice of God in the soul."* Indeed, everyone had a conscience, and it is one of the ways that you can receive the voice of God into your life. Apostle Paul writes in Romans 2:15-16, *"They show that the work of the law is written on their hearts, while their conscience also bears witness, and their conflicting thoughts accuse or even excuse them on that day when, according to my gospel, God judges the secrets of men by Christ Jesus."* When you study God's word, your conscience is sharpened and alert to spiritual frequency and ready to pick the voice of God. So, when you get to a juncture where there is no direct statement in scriptures about the issue, God speaks through your conscience to tell you what His plan is for you in that situation. So, you need to ensure that your conscience is alert and alive.

5. Through circumstances and the exhortations of other people.

Sometimes, when we don't receive God's voice in the Bible, God will create or allow challenging circumstances in our lives to get our attention and align us with His plan. So, you should not always interpret every event of your life as an attack from the devil. However, you need to train your spirit such that even if it's the devil, you can still hear God amid the storms around your life. In Act 9, there was a circumstance that God used to interrupt Saul's blood-thirsty agenda and aligned him in His plan and purpose.

So here is the point, an unending thirst for God's voice should be your greatest pursuit as you seek to journey in God's plan for your life.

CHAPTER 8

"HOW DO I HEAR FROM GOD?"

Every Christian has probably wondered at one time or another, "How do I hear from God?" The question is natural because we want to know what God has in store for us, and we are eager to please our heavenly Father. The range of answers, however, has caused much confusion and controversy. We need to be biblical when we answer the question, how can I hear from God?

The Bible tells us how we hear from God: "Long ago, at many times and in many ways, God spoke to our fathers by the prophets, but in these last days he has spoken to us by his Son, whom he appointed the heir of all things, through whom also he created the world" (Hebrews 1:1–2, ESV).

Before the Incarnation of God, the Son, God the Father spoke through the prophets. We heard from God through men such as Moses, Isaiah, Ezekiel, Micah, Malachi, and the other prophets. They relayed messages from God, and often their words were written down and preserved so we would always know His promises, His law, and His redemptive plans.

There were times when God spoke directly to people. Abraham and Joshua, for example, conversed with

God directly at times (Genesis 12:1; 17:1; Joshua 5:13–15). Others, such as Jacob, heard from God through dreams (Genesis 28:12–13). Ezekiel saw visions (Ezekiel 1:1). Saul began to hear from God and spoke for Him when "the Spirit of God came powerfully upon him" (1 Samuel 10:10).

But, in most cases, people did not hear from God directly; rather, they were responsible for reading God's written Word or seeking out God's chosen mouthpiece. On at least two occasions, King Jehoshaphat asked to hear from a prophet of God. The king of Israel requested that Jehoshaphat follow him to battle, but he needed to be sure that the battle would not be his last. So, he asked that a prophet be called to help them inquire from God how the battle will go.

"And Jehoshaphat said unto the king of Israel, Enquire, I pray thee, at the word of the LORD to day. Then the king of Israel gathered the prophets together, about four hundred men, and said unto them, Shall I go against Ramothgilead to battle, or shall I forbear? And they said, Go up; for the Lord shall deliver it into the hand of the king. And Jehoshaphat said, Is there not here a prophet of the LORD besides, that we might enquire of him?" 1 Kings 22:5-7

Also, Ben-Hadad, king of Aram, sought to hear from God through the prophet Elisha. Let's see 2 Kings 8:7-8, *"And Elisha came to Damascus; and Benhadad the king of Syria was sick; and it was told him, saying, The man of God is come hither. And the king said unto Hazael, Take a present in thine hand, and go, meet the man of God, and enquire of the LORD by him, saying, Shall I recover of this disease?"*

Isaiah told the people of Judah they had a responsibility to "consult God's instruction and the testimony of warning." Isaiah 8:20 says, *"To the law and to the testimony: if they speak not according to this word, it is because there is no light in them."* That is, they were to read the written Word of God, which has already been delivered to them, so they can find the solution to their challenges and answers to their questions.

However, with the birth of Jesus, things changed. John the Baptist was the last of the Old Testament prophets. Through the ministry of Jesus, God spoke directly to us. Jesus' teachings in the Sermon on the Mount, the Sermon on the Plain, and the Olivet Discourse; and His pronouncements of being the Bread of Life, the True Vine, and the Good Shepherd are God's direct revelation of who He is. Jesus' words "are full of the Spirit and life" (John 6:63).

The writer to the Hebrews says, "In these last days he has spoken to us by his Son." The "last days" are the current dispensation—the church age. Jesus Christ was the pinnacle of God's revelation; He is the Final Word to us. In the Bible, Jesus' words are recorded for us. When Jesus ascended back into heaven, He left behind hand-picked apostles who were given the special task of recording what Jesus had said and done. Under the inspiration of the Holy Spirit, these men were authorized by God to speak and record God's words to His church so that all of the church could truly hear from God. We now hear from God through His written Word, which is the Bible.

So, basically, we hear from God by reading our Bible and hearing it preached.

Many people who want to hear from God may not be satisfied reading the Bible. They desire more "direct" and "personal" communication with God aside from the written word. There are many problems with such a desire, starting with the fact that neglecting or rejecting the Bible to seek a "new" word from God is spiritually dangerous. I believe that it is arrogance for someone to think that he is so special as to receive direct revelation from God, especially when God said in scriptures that He has spoken through His Son, who is "appointed heir of all things, and through whom also he made the universe" (Hebrews 1:2). We can't stop Jesus. There are no modern-day apostles or prophets who function similarly as the biblical apostles and prophets.

God does speak to people today, but the means He uses always include the Bible. The Holy Spirit indwells every believer and gives gifts to them as He chooses. Some are given gifts to teach, correct, admonish, and encourage other Christians. There is no new revelation being given (see Revelation 22:18), but God has gifted people in the church to be able to speak into the lives of other Christians. Exhortation and the offering of biblical advice are important within the community of believers.

In addition to studying the Bible, there are also some ways to hear from God. The truth is, no one can box God; that is, you can't restrict God to a location. Also, a pastor's instruction from God's Word is one way we hear from God today. A friend's advice, tied to Scripture, is another way we hear from God. A directive issued by a God-ordained authority figure is another way we hear from God.

Now, let's examine some other ways to hear from God.

1. Through Praise and Worship

You see, praise is one of the ways to draw God's attention. The Bible says in Psalm 22:3, *"But thou art holy, O thou that inhabitest the praises of Israel."* God dwells in an atmosphere of praise and worship. And so, when you subscribe to praise and worship, you seamlessly enjoy His presence, and you can access His voice. For instance, the King of Judah and the King of Edom have struggled severally to get water for their land, but all to no avail. Then they came to Prophet Elisha to inquire of the Lord for the solution. But Elisha asked that a minstrel should play for Him; in other words, he needed an atmosphere of worship, and when she did, the Lord spoke, and the prophecy came to pass.

"But Jehoshaphat said, Is there not here a prophet of the LORD, that we may enquire of the LORD by him? And one of the king of Israel's servants answered and said, Here is

Elisha the son of Shaphat, which poured water on the hands of Elijah. And Elisha said, As the LORD of hosts liveth, before whom I stand, surely, were it not that I regard the presence of Jehoshaphat the king of Judah, I would not look toward thee, nor see thee. But now bring me a minstrel. And it came to pass, when the minstrel played, that the hand of the LORD came upon him. And he said, Thus saith the LORD, Make this valley full of ditches. For thus saith the LORD, Ye shall not see wind, neither shall ye see rain; yet that valley shall be filled with water, that ye may drink, both ye, and your cattle, and your beasts." 2 Kings 3:11, 14-17. Why not subscribe for a life of worship. In your car, on your way to the gym, during your workout, let the praise of God be always in your mouth, and you will keep hearing what God has to say.

2. Fasting and prayers.

The Bible says, ask, and you will receive, and one of the ways to hear from God is through prayers couple with fasting. God is not a taskmaster, He is your Father, and He wants to speak to you more than you want to hear from Him. For instance, the people of Israel, led by Ezra, needed to hear from God on the way to go and what they should do. And so proclaimed a fast, and they prayed to God, and He showed them the way. They needed to understand God's plan for their lives, and God revealed the answer.

Ezra 8:21-23, *"Then I proclaimed a fast there, at the river of Ahava, that we might afflict ourselves before our God, to seek of him a right way for us, and for our little ones, and for all our substance. For I was ashamed to require of the king a band of soldiers and horsemen to help us against the enemy in the way: because we had spoken unto the king, saying, The hand of our God is upon all them for good that seek him; but his power and his wrath is against all them that forsake him. So we fasted and besought our God for this: and he was intreated of us."*

3. Going to Church regularly.

David said in Psalm 73:17, *"Until I went into the sanctuary of God; then understood I their end."* In other words, there was a dimension of understanding that through God's voice that came when David appeared in the sanctuary. You see, you are missing a lot when you stay away from the church. There are diverse gifts and manifestations of the spirit that only happen when the saints gather. So, make out time to always be in church. Make it a duty as a family to always be in church. There you will know what God has ordained for you and what you need to do to maximize it.

CHAPTER 9

BENEFIT OF STUDYING GOD'S WORD

So, Beatrice got a new home appliance - a blender. So, she uses it for blending her vegetables only, unknown to her, that it has four other benefits apart from blending, but how would she know? How will she know when she didn't go through the manual that came with the blender, she just assumed that that's the only function the blender came with.

Just like Beatrice, how would you know God's plan for you when you've not read or studied His manual? How would you be enriched by God when you're void of His word? His word is key in fulfilling your plan, His word is pertinent to you being enriched, and you wouldn't be able to effectively know His plan for you if you're not acquainted with His word. Too often, people are self-encouraged to take action when exposed to what they stand to gain. So, what benefits come with studying God's word? Let's examine a few of them.

1. RECEIVE GUIDANCE

Your word is a lamp to my feet and a light to my path, **Psalm 119:105**

Guidance are instructions; they are lights on a man's path. A man without light might not accurately and precisely walk in the plan of God. Guidance is advice and counseling that will set one on the right path in life and destiny. And there's no place where you can get accurate guidance except in the word of God. The scripture says, in **Psalm 32:8**, *"I will instruct thee and teach thee in the way which thou shalt go: I will guide thee with mine eye."*

It is the word of God that guides a man into taking the right steps and decisions; without the word of God, you'd make decisions of your head knowledge, and it doesn't take one far, but with God's guidance, you'll go far.

Every way may look like *the way* to you when you don't know (Notice the phrase "the way"). Indeed, there's a way that you must walk in, and it is through guidance that you can know *the way*. *"And thine ears shall hear a word behind thee, saying, this is* **the way** *walk ye in it, when ye turn to the right hand, and when ye turn to the left.* **Isaiah 30:21.** An in-depth study of God's word guides you, directs your step, and sends light to your path in fulfilling your plan.

2. ANSWERED PRAYERS

If ye abide in me and my words abide in you, ye shall ask what ye will, and it shall be done unto you. **John 15:7**

We all love it when our prayers are answered, but getting your prayers answered is much easier when you pray according to God's word. One of the ways to get encouraged in your journey is to pray according to God's plan; it is there in you get a clue, a hint as to what he'll have you do per time and season. However, you can only pray accurately and get answers when you pray according to God's word.

You don't struggle with the prayers because you know God's word; all you need to do is affirm His word. Renounce the devil and His thoughts, bring to the negotiation table the word of the Lord, which is the power of the Lord. *"...For thou hast magnified thy word above all thy name"* **Psalm 138:2**

He has such a great name, but His word is exalted more than His name. However, you can only get this done by acquainting yourself with the word of God.

3. KNOWING GOD

And ye shall know the truth, and the truth shall set you free. **John 8:32**

You don't want to be in oblivion about the one in charge of your life; He has everything about you in His hands, he knows you more than you know yourself, but you must get to know him. In him, your reality lies; how then do you have access to your reality when you don't know who's in charge. How can you know when you've not read? Jesus said in **John 10:27,** *My sheep hear my voice, and I know them, and they follow me.*

Knowing a person's voice doesn't happen by chance.

You know there's this friend of yours when you hear them speak from afar, you know without anyone telling you that's your friend speaking. When you perceive a particular fragrance, you can link it to the fragrance of your friend. It happens because you have a close relationship with such a person; you follow them closely, you've learned their pros and cons, you've gotten acquainted with them.

This is the same with God; you must build a relationship with him to fulfill your plan, so you can know he's the one speaking at specific times, and you can differentiate His voice from that of others. To know God is to read God, and how do we read God… His word.

4. BUILDS UP YOUR FAITH

So then faith cometh by hearing, and hearing by the Word of God. **Romans 10:17**

As you journey to fulfill your God-ordained plans, some days will look blurry; you'd feel weary. Days so challenging, days that will look like God are not true; are not true; the amount of God's word that you have stored up will speak for you on such days.

How much of God's word you've read, heard, and digested will build your faith on a day like this. A man without enough and sufficient words will fall; the words must be readily available. They're the ones that will help you stand; it is those words that will build up your faith and cause you to forge on, soar and thrive.

How then do you build up your faith, when you've not learned the word of faith?

5. NOURISHMENT

But he answered and said, it is written, Man shall not live by bread alone, but by every word that proceedeth out of the mouth of God. **Matthew 4:4**

One astonishing thing that happens in the place of studying the word is that you're nourished. You're nourished for the journey ahead, just as it pertains to the natural man to feed on meals to keep living and nourished, so also is a man with a purpose who wants to walk in God's plan for his or her life. The Bible says in **1 Peter 2:2**, *As newborn babes, desire the sincere milk of the word, that we may grow thereby:*

You desire the word of the Lord to grow; it is in His that nourishment comes. You're nourished from all the world's deformities, your mind is renewed, and you're able to work in God's plan without you short-changing yourself fully.

6. EMPOWERMENT

He giveth power to the faint; and to them that have no might he increaseth strength. **Isaiah 40:29**

In God's word, you get empowered; it's in His word that you get re-energized. God's plan for your life is too big for you; you can't carry it yourself. But he will empower you. How will He? Through His words. Empowerment will come to you through the word of

God. Your visions are no longer clouded or blurry; you can see clearly because His words bring to light.

Psalm 121:1 says, *I'll lift up mine eyes unto the hills from whence cometh my help.*

Empowerment is help, your help comes from God, and it comes through His word

7. HEALING

For I will restore health unto thee, and I will heal thee of thy wounds, saith the Lord; because they called there an outcast, saying this is Zion, whom no man seeketh after. **Jeremiah 30:17**

Most people in the process of following their wisdom and knowledge without God have fallen into error and unpleasant situations. We now have injuries here and there, spiritual wounds, emotional wounds, career wounds, and many other wounds. But in God's word, that's where healing resides. One who's sick can't accurately walk in God's will for his or her life, so it's expedient for you to heal up.

Psalms 147:3 says, He healeth the broken in heart, and bindeth up their wounds. So, to move up with the plan of God for your life, you must first heal up; you must heal up from past disappointments, past hurt, past loss, and several others. It is only in the word of God that you can get the healing your soul desires. God heals; His word heals because His word is life and truth.

8. CORRECTION

All scripture is given by inspiration of God, and is profitable for doctrine, for reproof, for correction, for instruction in righteousness: that the man of God may be perfect, thoroughly furnished unto all good works. **2 Timothy 3:16-17**

A compelling benefit of studying God's word is for correction and reproof. In the course of the journey to your destination, there are days you'd make mistakes. And when a man makes mistakes, and he's not corrected, what he'll achieve at the end of the journey will not be plausible if he furthers on with the journey. But if he makes mistakes, come back, learns, and works with the experience gathered from the previous mistakes, such a man is on a bright part.

Search me, o God, and know my heart: try me and know my thoughts: and see if there be any wicked way in me, and lead me in the way everlasting. **Psalm 139:23-24**

The word of God purges you, purifies you, and refines you like a refiner. His word opens your eyes to things you never knew were wrong, and you've been doing, thereby restricting you from walking accurately in His plan. His word searches you and removes the blindfold off your eyes; His word reduces your terrain of ignorance, thereby giving you the power to possess your possessions as ordained from the beginning.

9. FREEDOM

And ye shall know the truth and the truth shall set you free. **John 8:32**

Freedom comes from the word of God; you can't successfully execute the plan of God for your life in bondage. The word of the Lord is where liberation lies, total freedom. You're not in the bondage of your past; you're not in the bondage of your foundation; you're free because He has set you free.

If the Son therefore makes you free, ye shall be free indeed. **John 8:36**

Freedom is gotten in the place of studying God's word because the word in itself is freedom.

10. COMMITMENT

Commit your works to the Lord. And your plans will be established. **Psalm 37:5**

This is a pertinent benefit of studying God's word. Through His word, you learn commitment. You learn to be committed to the plan he has placed in your hands, and you also know that nothing committed into His hands fails. When you study the scripture, you'll find out that all through Jesus's journey on earth, He was committed. He was committed and always making reference to His Father in heaven; while he was at the point of crucifixion, it was difficult, and he said,

"... O my father, if it be possible, let this cup pass from me: nevertheless not as I will, but as thou wilt". **Matthew 26:39**

He was committed till the point of crucifixion, such commitments you learn from different patriarchs of old when you sit with the word. And on days when you're feeble, the words you've garnered from the word of God begin to subconsciously take charge of you and give you the grace to pull through.

But Jesus said to him, "No one, after putting His hand to the plough and looking back, is fit for the kingdom of God." **Luke 9:62**

You'd understand that the father seeks men who will be committed to the plan and the blueprint handed on to them without wavering or looking back.

11. JOY

Thou wilt shew me the path of life: in the presence is fullness of joy; at thy right hand there are pleasures forever more. **Psalm 16:11**

Joy is an embodiment of God's word; the word of the Lord carries joy. You can't study God's word and be gloomy; you can't dine with the king of joy, the one who has everlasting joy in His custody and the feeling of His presence doesn't run off on you. To fulfill that plan, you need the joy of Christ, which can only be gotten from consistent studying of His word.

When you study God's word, it shows that either you've attained the goal, it doesn't look like you're getting there anytime soon, or the road is looking all sloppy, you'd still rejoice. Because he doesn't fail, His words assure you that he doesn't have the luxury to fail, and He is working things out for you, so all you need to do is rejoice.

Paul said in **1 Thessalonians 5:16,** *Rejoice evermore.*

The word of the Lord gives you the assurance and reassurance that you haven't gotten there, but right on your way, there's no cause for alarm because he got you. Rejoice!!!

12. IMPACT

Let the word of Christ dwell in you richly in all wisdom; teaching and admonishing one another in psalms and hymns and spiritual songs, singing with grace in your hearts to the Lord. **Colossians 3:16**

A maxim says, "you can't give what you don't have." Yes, it's very true, you'd only be able to give what you have, and you know that you have it. One thing is that the word of the Lord doesn't hoard itself. You'll want to talk about it; you begin to live by it, make reference to it, and do everything by it, thereby impacting several other lives.

The word of the Lord becomes your mantra and to walk in the father's will and plan becomes easier becomes you have several others you're leading and teaching on the journey.

You give out all you've studied, and it's imminent and necessary to go and read up, feed on more words so as not to be empty but to recharge, keep on blessing lives and not being a parasite by just feeding but that gentiles come to your light and Kings to the rising of your brightness. The impact you need resides in the word of the Lord.

13. PEACE

And the peace of God, which passeth all understanding, shall keep your hearts and minds through Christ Jesus.
Philippians 4:7

Peace is a driving force in fulfilling God's plan for your life. You're rest assured of tomorrow; there's no fear, the economy is melting down, you're not bothered, Issues arising from here and there, but you're strong in the Lord because he has given you peace and rest on all sides. The peace of the Lord is only gotten from His word; when His peace journeys with you, you're less worried or anxious.

These and many more benefit from studying God's word as a prerequisite to understanding God's ultimate plan for your life and fulfilling them. You should always remember that you don't go wrong with God's word; never, you don't. It's the compass of your soul if you subscribe fully to it and to its demands.

CHAPTER 10

WHO KNOWS TOMORROW?

How often have you wondered if only you could know exactly what tomorrow holds? The best of technologies today can only forecast and predict what will happen tomorrow. Still, no one has been able to develop an application that can certainly tell what the future holds. In the same vein, some people even ask if God knows the future.

You see, the Bible is always completely accurate, including its prophetic content. Consider, for instance, the prophecy that Christ would be born in Bethlehem of Judea, as foretold in Micah 5:2. Micah gave his prophecy around 700 B.C. Where was Christ born seven centuries later? In Bethlehem of Judea (Luke 2:1-20; Matthew 2:1-12).

Peter Stoner, in Science Speaks, has shown that the science of probability rules out coincidence in prophetic Scripture. Taking just eight prophecies concerning Christ, Stoner found that the chance that anyone man might have fulfilled all eight prophecies is 1 in 10 to the 17th power. That would be 1 chance in 100,000,000,000,000,000. Of course, Jesus fulfilled many more than eight prophecies! There is no doubt that Bible is totally accurate in foretelling the future.

Since He can foretell the future, God certainly knows the future. Isaiah recorded these words about God: *"Remember the former things long past, for I am God, and there is no other; I am God, and there is no one like Me, declaring the end from the beginning, and from ancient times things which have not been done, saying, 'My purpose will be established, and I will accomplish all My good pleasure"* (Isaiah 46:9-10). God is the only One who can stand at the beginning and accurately declare the end.

God is omniscient; He knows everything actual and possible. God is also eternal (Psalm 90:2). As the eternal, omniscient God, He has lived our yesterday, today, and tomorrow, the past, present, and future. God is the Alpha and Omega, the Beginning, and the End (Revelation 21:6).

There are still prophecies in the Bible that await fulfillment. Because God knows the future, we can count on the prophecies to eventually be fulfilled. Events are taking place in God's calendar according to His plan. We know who holds the future—the one true, personal, eternal, and all-knowing God of the Bible.

Securing the Future

Since God is the one who knows and holds the future, it is important to understand how we can secure our future in Him. Ordinarily, we could actually use it to walk through life based on assumptions and speculations. As human beings, we could decide to use our own knowledge to plan for the future.

We could consider ourselves smart enough to figure it all out. After all, we could see ourselves as educated, well-informed, and well-suited to handle the future. Unfortunately, things don't always go as planned. And if the cafe is not taken, we could be exposing ourselves to unnecessary frustrations.

The Bible describes the story of a man who thought he could sort everything out all by himself. He felt he had all that it would take. It seemed as though he had it all fine till something higher than him happened.

Luke 12:16 - 20:

16 Then He spoke a parable to them, saying: "The ground of a certain rich man yielded plentifully.

17 And he thought within himself, saying, 'What shall I do, since I have no room to store my crops?'

18 So he said, 'I will do this: I will pull down my barns and build greater, and there I will store all my crops and my goods.

19 And I will say to my soul, "Soul, you have many goods laid up for many years; take your ease; eat, drink, and be merry."'

20 But God said to him, 'Fool! This night your soul will be required of you; then whose will those things be which you have provided?'

He was a rich man. It seemed he must have been planning well prior to that time for him to have had such good results in his life. So, in this story, he was about to make "future" plans with all audacity, as if he knew what the future looked like.

He had long-term goals. He had big dreams. However, they never got to materialize. The same day he had those intentions was the same day his soul was required of him.

Why did that happen to him? He had not secured the future. We can only secure the future by walking hand-in-hand with the One who holds the future.

Jesus admonished us that we should not be anxious about the future and get ourselves stressed up about it. We are rather supposed to stay in touch with God. By doing so, the future will be well under control.

Matthew 6:33-34 says

33 But seek first the kingdom of God and His righteousness, and all these things shall be added to you.

34 Therefore do not worry about tomorrow, for tomorrow will worry about its own things. Sufficient for the day is its own trouble.

We can then see that in planning for the future, we have to seek God. We should allow Him to be the one to take us through the journey. He is the one who knows the way. It is worth it to depend on Him and trust Him to lead us on.

There are things ahead which we cannot see. Our eyes can only see so far; they cannot see all. His own eyes can see farther; they can see all. He knows how to navigate our future. Relying on Him is the best way we can secure the future.

Fulfilling the Future

Whether one depends on God for the future or not, there is a role to play. Everybody has to work diligently to make the best out of life.

However, we want to see how to realize that God knows tomorrow to whatever we do. We need to know how we can fulfill the future according to the will of God.

We cannot afford to walk through life's journey without actively involving God. That would be too costly. Apostle James admonished us on this.

James 4:13-15

13 Come now, you who say, "Today or tomorrow we will go to such and such a city, spend a year there, buy and sell, and make a profit";

14 whereas you do not know what will happen tomorrow. For what is your life? It is even a vapor that appears for a little time and then vanishes away.

15 Instead you ought to say, "If the Lord wills, we shall live and do this or that."

We can see that involving God in all we want to do, is indispensable. Actually, God is not against our heart desires. The only issue is that those desires might not come to pass since we are not the ones controlling every situation.

However, by considering God, we can have things go

on fine for us. He knows how to make things work out no matter what comes our way.

Proverbs 3:5-7

5 Trust in the Lord with all your heart,

And lean not on your own understanding;

6 In all your ways acknowledge Him,

And He shall direct your paths.

7 Do not be wise in your own eyes...

We are to trust in the Lord with all our hearts. Since He is the only one who knows the future, we can trust His knowledge and judgments. Since He is the only one who holds the future, we can trust His ability to lead the way.

If we will acknowledge Him in all our ways, He can direct our paths. We should not be wise in our own eyes. We need to partner with God, so we can fulfill the future.

Psalm 37:4 - 5

4 Delight yourself also in the Lord,

And He shall give you the desires of your heart.

5 Commit your way to the Lord,

Trust also in Him, And He shall bring it to pass.

Our beautiful desires and dreams about the future can come to pass. Of course, it is not everybody that gets their dreams fulfilled. Several challenges in life could make things turn out adversely. But for us, there is a way to live above this.

The Bible tells us we should delight ourselves in the Lord. This means we put Him as our priority. That means we are so committed to Him that we full assurance in Him. He would therefore grant the desires of our hearts.

As we continually commit our ways to Him, and trust Him, He will make our plans come to pass. Though we don't know the future, we are not disturbed. The famous Christian quote captures this so well: "I DO NOT KNOW WHAT THE FUTURE HOLDS, BUT I KNOW THE ONE WHO HOLDS THE FUTURE." We can expect the very best as we choose to follow God in this journey.

CHAPTER 11

KEEPER OF COVENANTS

We live in a time when there is a high level of uncertainty. People go to work and are unsure if the management will lay them off any time soon. People in business monitor the stock exchange every minute to see if they still have a chance of making a profit. The court is filled with people who aren't interested in keeping their marriage vows. Friends now sign binding contracts before starting a business deal. Indeed, man is one of the most unstable creatures in the universe.

While growing up, most parents rain promises for their children that they can't even meet up with. Husband's confidently read out vows to his lovely bride, and a few years down the line, his reactions are far from what he promised. I understand you may have trusted people, and they let you down at the last moment. You may have even made up your mind never to hold on to anyone's words anymore.

Yes, I understand that feeling perfectly, and I assume you may also wonder if it's okay to believe that God has a plan to enrich you. You may ask yourself." Does God change His mind?" "Does He stick to His plans as He has written?" Perhaps you have taken up the challenge to always study the bible, and ever since, you have discovered great plans that God has mapped for you and your generation. Yet the thought still comes, "Will God really do all these things that He has said?"

Now, let's read this verse about our Heavenly Father; Malachi 3:6 says, *"I the LORD do not change. So, you, O descendants of Jacob, are not destroyed."* This is God assuring the children of Israel and, by extension, you, of His inability to change, especially His words towards you. Similarly, James 1:17 tells us, *"Every good and perfect gift is from above, coming down from the Father of the heavenly lights, who does not change like shifting shadows."* Nothing is as constant as God and His operations among men. He is not subject to circumstances, nor is he limited by event and nature.

If men have let you down, there is hope in a God that is not man. The bible says in Numbers 23:19, *"God is not a man, that He should lie, nor a son of man, that He should change His mind. Does He speak and then not act? Does He promise and not fulfill?"* Did you get that?

What God has said about you is as sure as the break of day. He is not the boss that promised to promote you and later changed His mind. He is not your parents who plan to take you on vacation, and excuse not doing so. He is not your spouse who forgot he vowed to love you till death. The Bible verse is clear that man is limited in his attempt to do all that he promises to do. There is a system in man that ensures that sometimes he doesn't deliver on his words and plans. But not God.

God does not change. God is unchanging and unchangeable. He is also all-wise. So, He cannot "change His mind" in the sense of realizing a mistake, backtracking, and trying a new tack. God knows that you have had several disappointments with men, so the bible started by making a clear distinction that God is not a man that He should lie. So, you can bank on His word and expect the delivery. All through, we have x-rayed the plans of God for your life, and among them is to enrich you, and if you have ever doubted this, then it's time to change your mind. It's time to sit up and know that God's plan for, you is sure.

Now let me open this truth up even wider. God is so sure of bringing His plan to pass in your life that He didn't just leave it hanging as a promise, but He went further to strike an agreement with you and called it a covenant. In other words, if you think I am not serious about making you a billionaire, if you doubt my plan to lift you and make you a blessing to many people, families, and nations, let me strike an irrevocable covenant with you.

Let's see what he said about David in Psalm 89:34-37,

"My covenant will I not break, nor alter the thing that is gone out of my lips. Once have I sworn by my holiness that I will not lie unto David. His seed shall endure for ever, and his throne as the sun before me. It shall be established for ever as the moon, and as a faithful witness in heaven."

He disclosed His plan to David that his descendants

shall always be on the throne in Israel. And he sealed it by a covenant. That's the God we serve. He doesn't joke with words. In fact, the Psalmist said in Psalm 138:2, *"I will worship toward thy holy temple, and praise thy name for thy lovingkindness and for thy truth: for thou hast magnified thy word above all thy name."* He monitors His words and His plans even more than His name.

You may ask, "How then do we explain verses that seem to say that God does change His mind?" Such as Genesis 6:6, *"The LORD was grieved that He had made man on the earth, and His heart was filled with pain."* Also, Exodus 32:14 proclaims, *"Then the LORD relented and did not bring on His people the disaster He had threatened."* These verses speak of the Lord "repenting" or "relenting" of something and seem to contradict the doctrine of God's immutability.

Another passage that is often used to show that God changes His mind is the story of Jonah. Through His prophet, God had told Nineveh He would destroy the city in forty days (Jonah 3:4). However, Nineveh repented of their sin (verses 5–9). In response to the Assyrians' repentance, God relented: "He had compassion and did not bring upon them the destruction He had threatened" (verse 10).

There are two important considerations involving the passages that say God changed His mind. First, we can say statements such as "the LORD was grieved that He had made man on the earth" (Genesis 6:6) are examples of anthropopathism (or anthropopathic).

Anthropopathism is a figure of speech in which finite humanity's feelings or thought processes are ascribed to the infinite God. It's a way to help us understand God's work from a human perspective. In Genesis 6:6 specifically, we know God's sorrow over man's sin. God obviously did not reverse His decision to create man. The fact that we are alive today is proof that God did not "change His mind" about the creation.

Furthermore, we must distinguish between conditional declarations of God and unconditional determinations of God. In other words, when God said, "I will destroy Nineveh in forty days," He was speaking conditionally upon the Assyrians' response. We know this because the Assyrians repented, and God did not mete out the judgment. God did not change His mind; instead, His message to Nineveh was a warning meant to provoke repentance, and His warning was successful.

An example of an unconditional declaration of God is the Lord's promise to David, *"Your house and your kingdom will endure forever before me; your throne will be established forever"* (2 Samuel 7:16). Here, there is no qualification expressed or implied in this declaration. No matter what David did or did not do, the word of the Lord would come to pass.

God tells us of the cautionary nature of some of His declarations and the fact that He will act in accordance with our choices: "If at any time I announce that a nation or kingdom is to be uprooted, torn down and destroyed, and if that nation I warned repents of its evil, then I will relent and not inflict on it the disaster I had planned. And if at another time I announce that a nation or kingdom is to be built up and planted, and if it does evil in my sight and does not obey me, then I will reconsider the good I had intended to do for it.

"Now therefore say to the people of Judah and those living in Jerusalem, 'This is what the Lord says: Look! I am preparing a disaster for you and devising a plan against you. So, turn from your evil ways, each one of you, and reform your ways and your actions" (Jeremiah 18:7– 11).

Note the conditional word if: "If that nation I warned repents [like Assyria in Jonah 3] . . . then I will relent." Conversely, God may tell a nation they will be blessed, but "if it does evil in my sight [like Israel in Micah 1] ... then I will reconsider the good I had intended to do."

The bottom line is that God is entirely consistent. In His Holiness, God was going to judge Nineveh. However, Nineveh repented and changed its ways. As a result, God, in His Holiness, had mercy on Nineveh and spared them. This "change of mind" is entirely consistent with His character. His Holiness did not waver one iota.

The fact that God changes His treatment of us in response to our choices has nothing to do with His character. In fact, because God does not change, He must treat the righteous differently from the unrighteous. If someone repents, God consistently forgives; if someone refuses to repent, God always judges. He is unchanging in His nature, His plan, and His being. He cannot one day be pleased with the contrite and be angry with the contrite the next day. That would show Him to be mutable and untrustworthy. For God to tell Nineveh, "I'm going to judge you," and then (after they repent) refuse to judge them may look like God changed His mind. In reality, God was simply staying true to His character. He loves mercy and forgives the penitent. "Has God forgotten to be merciful?" (Psalm 77:9). The answer is no.

At one time, we were all enemies of God due to our sin (Romans 8:7). God warned us of the wages of sin (Romans 6:23) to cause us to repent. When we repented and trusted Christ for salvation, God "changed His mind" about us, and now we are no longer enemies but His beloved children (John 1:12). As it would be contrary to God's character not to punish us had we continued in sin, so it would be contrary to His character to punish us after we repented. Does our change of heart mean that God changes? No, if anything, our salvation points to the fact that God does not change because had He not saved us for the sake of Christ, He would have acted contrary to His character

Friend, what has God told you? Which of His promises have you seen while reading this book or studying your bible? I want you to know that God is committed to bringing it to pass. He is a covenant-keeping God; that's why you can sleep and wake on His promises. You can freely declare His plans to enrich you and increase you every day without fear of being let down halfway. God is too faithful to fail you.

You Have a Part In It

However, as great and assuring as God's covenant are, you have a part to play. Yes, every one of His promises leaves you with a responsibility. Every covenant has a condition that you must meet before it can take effect in your life. God is always faithful on His own part, and it is important we must be faithful on our own part if we must enjoy the benefits of the covenant.

The plan of God for your life will always leave you with what to do. We have discussed how valid and unchanging God's part is in the deal, but my question to you is, do you know your part? Have you found out what you need to do as part of God's covenant?

For instance, God declared His plan in Deuteronomy 28:1-6, *"And it shall come to pass, if thou shalt hearken diligently unto the voice of the LORD thy God, to observe and to do all his commandments which I command thee this day, that the LORD thy God will set thee on high above all nations of the earth: And all these blessings shall come on thee, and overtake thee, if thou shalt hearken unto the voice of the LORD thy God. Blessed shalt thou be in the city, and blessed shalt thou be in the field. Blessed shall be the fruit of thy body, and the fruit of thy ground, and the fruit of thy cattle, the increase of thy kine, and the flocks of thy sheep. Blessed shall be thy basket and thy store. Blessed shalt thou be when thou comest in, and blessed shalt thou be when thou goest out."*

If you read further, you will see that the blessings continue. As great as this plan is, it started with your part. You need to obey God. You need to trust God and follow His instructions. He has ordained to enrich you, but are you prepared to take delivery of that wealth? Are you ready to obtain what He has planned for you?

You see, once you have played your part, then the blessings begin to flow ceaselessly. So, whenever you study the Bible from now, search for areas where you need to be committed. Ask questions, "What's my part in this covenant of prosperity?" "What should I keep doing to succeed in my business?" As long as you remain committed to doing it, rest assured that what God has said will surely come to pass in your life. What He has planned will become a reality in your life.

CONCLUSION

I want you to understand that you are here for a purpose, and the fulfillment of that purpose should be your priority. God has vowed to enrich you so that you can be a blessing to His work on the earth and to people around you. So, get excited!

It's time to launch deeper in your walk with God and develop a renewed intimacy with the Holy Spirit. Why? God's word says in Deuteronomy 29:29, *"The secret things belong unto the LORD our God: but those things which are revealed belong unto us and to our children for ever, that we may do all the words of this law."* You need to know before you possess.

Your riches are not next week; your wealth is not next year, but right now. God has planned it all and as you align with His word, your life shall begin to manifest His riches.

www.ingramcontent.com/pod-product-compliance
Lightning Source LLC
Chambersburg PA
CBHW071717040426
42446CB00011B/2099